Dessert Party

Dessert Party

Bake, Decorate & Entertain with Over 50 Easy-to-Bake Recipes   www.dessertparty.net

FIRST PUBLISHED SEPTEMBER 2014
COPYRIGHT © 2014 BY HOURGLASS PRESS LLC.

All rights reserved. No part of this book may be reproduced or transmitted in any form or by any digital, electronic or mechanical means, including information storage and retrieval systems, without prior written permission of the publisher.

Hourglass Press LLC.
902 Broadway, 14th Floor
New York, NY 10010
www.hourglasspress.com

Text © 2014 by Patricia Cartin
Editorial Direction: Susan Lauzau Editorial Services
Design & Illustrations © 2014 by: CORAL Communications & Design
www.coralcommunicationsdesign.com
Art Direction: Carol Guzowski
Photography: Elizabeth Yuna Kim
Layout & Illustrations: Elizabeth Yuna Kim
Design Assistant & Photo Editor: Saul Suaza
Baking Asistant: Alexandra Matsu

This book is a single component of DESSSERT PARTY and is not intended to be sold separately.
First edition, Paperback, September 2014
ISBN: 978-1-935682-13-4
Library of Congress Cataloging-in-Publication data available upon request.
09/14; 10 9 8 7 6 5 4 3 2 1
Printed and Manufactured in China

Please note: The publisher has made every effort to ensure the accuracy of the text, and every recipe in this book has been home-tested in an effort to assure that the information contained within is correct. Variations in consistencies will occur depending on altitude and experience; we encourage you to practice, practice, and enjoy!

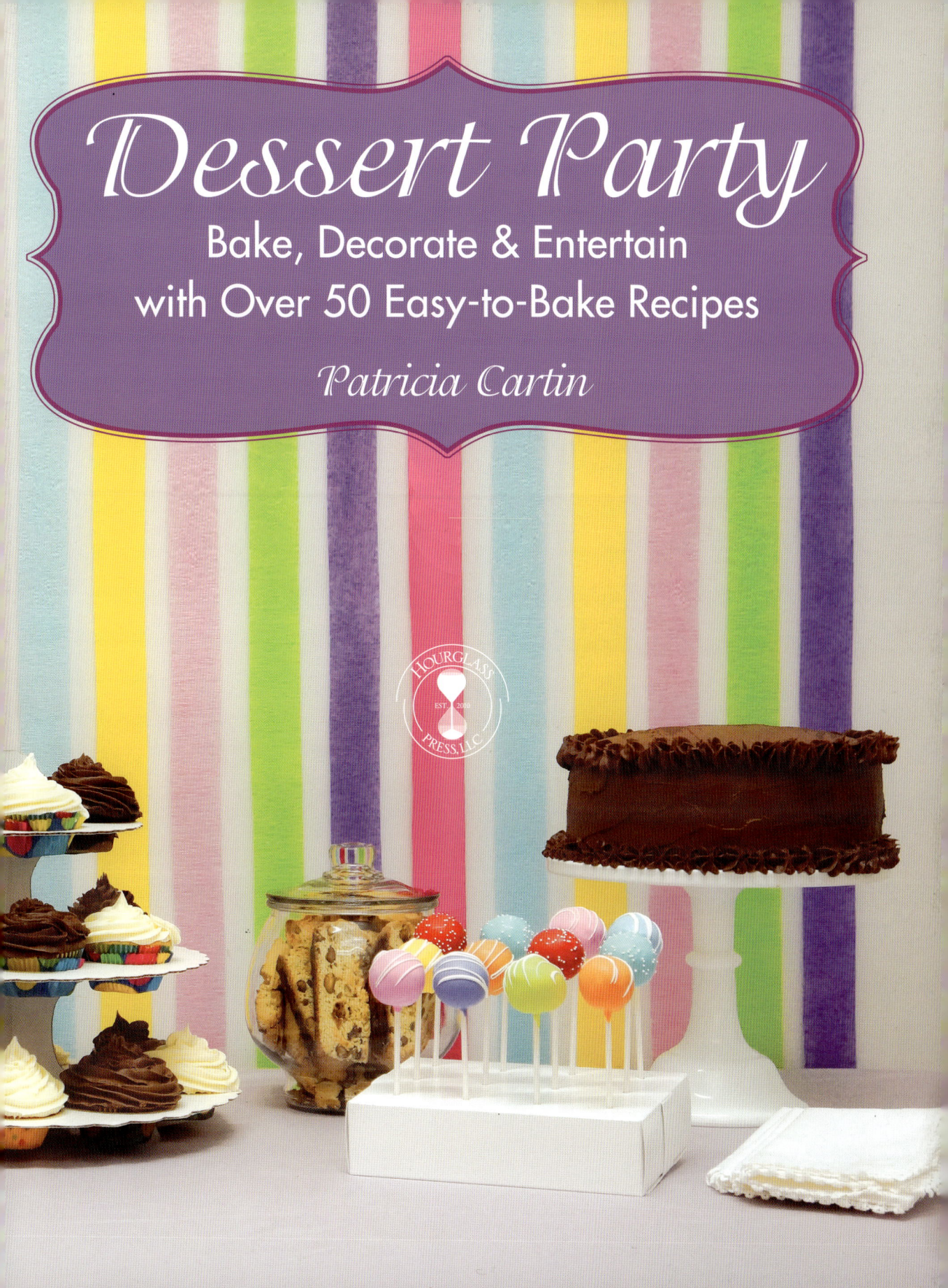

CONTENTS

Introduction 7

THE BASICS

Ingredients 8
Measuring 10
Beating Eggs 10
Mixing 11
Folding 12
Melting Chocolate 13
Baking 14
Unmolding a Baked Cake 14
Baking Pans 15
Other Equipment 15
Icing Cakes 16
Other Icing Techniques 17
Cutting Cake 17
Icing Cupcakes 18
Coloring Icing 19
Stands 20
Happy Baking! 21

CAKES

Devil's Food Cake 25
Chocolate Almond Mini Cakes 27
Chocolate Chip Cake 28
Vanilla Cake with Mocha Icing 29
Golden Cake with Buttercream and Walnuts 31
Sponge Cake with Strawberries and
  Whipped Cream 33
Coconut Layer Cake 35
German Chocolate Coconut Layer Cake 37
Caramel Cake 39
Carrot Cake with Cream Cheese Frosting 41
Green Grapes Cake 43
Apricot Upside Down Cake 45
Apple Cake 47
Orange-Nut Cake with Cointreau Syrup 49

CUPCAKES

Super-Rich Chocolate Cupcakes 53
Chocolate-Orange Cupcakes 55
Cupcakes with Sour Cream and Raisins 57
Red Velvet Cupcakes 59
Vanilla Cupcakes 61
Chai Cupcakes 63

COOKIES

Chocolate Thumbprint Cookies with
  Strawberry Jelly 67
Brownie Crinkles 68
White Chocolate Cookies 69
Mixed-Chip Cookies 71
Oatmeal-Raisin Cookies 73
Peanut Butter Cookies 75
Sour Cream Cookies 76
Spicy Dark Chocolate Cookies 77
Ebony and Ivory Spirals and Marbles 79
Delicate Almond Cookies 81
Zesty Lemon Stars 84
Linzer Hearts with Raspberry Jam 85
Butter Cookies 87
Black and White Sugar Cookies 89
Gingerbread Cookies 91
Sugar Cookie Cream Sandwiches 93

BISCOTTI & BARS

Cinnamon and Coffee Bars 97
Brownie Bars with Fudge Icing 99
Coconut-Toffee Bars 100
Classic Chocolate Brownies 101
Cranberry-Orange Shortbreads 103
Chocolate-Dipped Nut Biscotti 105
Pistachio Biscotti 107

CAKE POPS

Chocolate Cake Pops 111
Vanilla Cake Pops 113

FROSTINGS & SAUCES

Cointreau Syrup 116
Vanilla Glaze 117
Cream Cheese Frosting 118
Whipped Cream 119
Vanilla Filling Cream 120
Easy Buttercream Frosting 121
Fluffy White Meringue 122
Confectioner's Sugar 123
Classic Cake Frosting 124
Honey Whipped Cream 125
Choco-Mint Icing 126
Mocha Frosting 127
Maple Frosting 128
Rich Caramel Sauce 129
Creamy Chocolate Frosting 130
Fudge Icing 131
Spreadable Chocolate Frosting 132
Ganache 133
German Chocolate Frosting 134
Chocolate Glaze 135

About the Author 136
Appendix 137
Index 140
Dedication 144

INTRODUCTION

My passion for baking started when I was six, in a small town called San Jose in Costa Rica. One day, I walked into my house after school and was captivated by the delicious aromas that took me straight to the kitchen. My mom was cooking something in a huge pot on the stove. Possibly, the pot only looked so big because I was so small. Seeing my curiosity, my mother told me she was making rice pudding. She stood me on a stepstool and gave me a wooden spoon so I could help. Standing high on the stool, I could see into the pot, as swirling cinnamon mingled with boiling milk and sugar. I never quite lost the enthusiasm I found that day, and it has turned into a lifelong passion for baking and cooking.

My purpose in writing this book is to share with you easy-to-bake recipes for delicious desserts I have enjoyed making for my own family and friends. I've selected these recipes with special care and affection, choosing those that bring great reward for a modicum of effort.

There is nothing more inviting than a home where something is baking. The scents draw us inside and assure us that we are cared for. It is said that baking is an art in which the first ingredient is love—there is no secret recipe, but only good ingredients that combine with love to produce unforgettable treats.

THE BASICS

Before you start any baking project, read the recipe through to make sure that you have on hand all the ingredients, pans, and utensils you will need. For every recipe, dairy ingredients and eggs should be brought to room temperature before using, while some recipes call for dough to be chilled for a period of time before baking. Organizing your ingredients and understanding the process ahead of time will help you make the most of your time and will yield the most delicious and consistent results.

Ingredients

In baking, ingredients are very important. All should be fresh and of good quality.

Eggs, butter, and milk should be brought to room temperature before you use them—room-temperature ingredients emulsify more readily, producing lighter and more evenly baked treats. Using cold ingredients may result in lumpy batters that yield denser, heavier cakes and cookies. Take your ingredients out of the rerigerator thirty minutes to an hour before you plan to begin baking—the timing will depend on the temperature of your home as well as the starting temperature of the ingredients.

If you are short on time, you can hasten the warming process a bit. Cut butter into small chunks and microwave for a few seconds at a time until it's just turning soft. Place cold eggs in warm—not hot—water for fifteen minutes. Heat milk in the microwave for ten seconds, repeating as needed, to take the chill off the milk.

Always use unsalted butter for baking, and use large eggs, unless the recipe specifies otherwise.

Dry ingredients such as flour, white sugar, confectioners' sugar, baking soda, baking powder, and so on should be sifted to remove any lumps and to add air into the granules. In addition, many recipes in this book call for certain ingredients to be sifted together, which allows the dry ingredients to blend before they are added to a mixture, promoting more even distribution.

Use all-purpose white flour, unless the recipe calls for a different flour mix.

When a recipe calls simply for sugar, I am referring to granulated white sugar. Brown sugar and confectioners' sugar (also called powdered sugar) are specified. Unless otherwise noted, "brown sugar" refers to light brown sugar; dark brown sugar has a higher moisture content that can alter the texture of baked goods.

BROWN SUGAR

WHITE SUGAR

CONFECTIONERS' SUGAR

    The recipes in this book were developed using table salt; note that Kosher salt and sea salt have coarser grains than table salt, so substitutions will alter the proportion unless you calculate carefully based on the type of salt you are using. For this reason, I recommend using regular table salt for these recipes.

    Baking powder and baking soda help baked goods rise because they form carbon dioxide when they come into contact with liquid and heat. Though both baking soda and baking powder will keep for a long time on pantry shelves, it's important that these ingredients are still potent when you use them—if they're not, your baked goods will turn out flat and heavy. If you're in doubt about their effectiveness, you can test them easily. For baking powder, just drop ¼ teaspoon into ½ cup of hot tap water; the baking powder should begin to effervesce immediately. Testing baking soda requires the addition of an acid: stir ¼ teaspoon of vinegar into the ½ cup hot water before adding the baking soda. If the baking powder or baking soda does not bubble on contact with the liquid, or if the reaction seems lazy, make a visit to the store for a fresh container.

    Chocolate is a centerpiece of many recipes in this book. Be sure to use the type of chocolate or cocoa specified in the recipe, so that the dessert is not overly sweet. Some recipes call for semisweet chocolate, while others call for unsweetened, and yet others for sweetened. Refer to page 13 for more about melting chocolate.

Measuring

In baking, measuring ingredients carefully is critical. Cooking is more forgiving, but many baking recipes depend upon precise measurements for the best results. Scoop flour loosely into the proper measure (1 cup, ½ cup, etc.), then pass a knife across the top of the cup to remove any excess. Granulated white sugar and confectioners' should be measured in the same manner. Brown sugar must be packed densely into the proper measuring cup before the knife is passed across the top.

In this book, measurements for butter are typically given in cups, and where applicable, the number of sticks needed is given for easy measuring.

It is simplest to measure liquids in a clear glass measuring cup, as you can set it on a level surface and see that the amount is exact. The spout on the cup makes for a neat pouring.

Beating Eggs

When beating whole eggs, crack the egg gently on a flat surface and let the egg drop from the shell into a mixing bowl. Be careful that no bits of shell get into the cracked eggs. Using an electric mixer, gradually increase the speed until it has reached the maximum, and continue beating on high until the eggs reach a thick consistency and are lighter in color. Once the eggs are thick and frothy, slow the mixing speed and gradually incorporate ingredients as indicated.

Separating Eggs

There are many ways to separate eggs. Here is the method I prefer: break the egg gently on a flat surface. Over a small bowl, pry the halves of the egg apart with your thumbs, being sure to let the yolk settle into the bottom half. The egg white will overflow into the bowl. Carefully transfer the yolk back and forth a few times between the two shell halves, allowing the white to drip into the bowl. Save the yolks in a separate bowl.

Beating Egg Whites

Before beating egg whites, make sure there are no bits of yolk or shell in the whites; yolk in the whites prevents them from achieving proper volume. Place the whites in a mixing bowl and, using an electric mixer, start increasing the speed gradually until you are at the maximum speed. Continue mixing at high speed until stiff peaks form in the whites. Do not overmix, as the white will turn liquid again. As soon as glossy peaks form, slow the mixing speed and gradually add the sugar, caramel, or whatever the recipe calls for. Then turn up the mixing speed to incorporate all ingredients well.

Beating Egg Yolks

First, make sure that no egg whites got into the yolks. Place the yolks in a mixing bowl and gradually increase the speed on your electric mixer until you have reached maximum speed. Continue beating the yolks until they become thick and lighten in color. When the yolks are thick and lemon yellow, add ingredients as specified by the recipe.

Mixing

Whether you are preparing a cake or cupcakes, beat the butter well first using an electric mixer and then add the sugar gradually until the two ingredients are well combined. Then start adding the eggs one by one and beat well after the addition of each egg, until the mixture is creamy. This process can take from ten to fifteen minutes. For most recipes, after the butter, sugar, and eggs are mixed together, dry ingredients are added, alternating with liquid ingredients.

Cookie recipes need slightly different treatment, as cookie dough is stiffer than cake batter. Beat the butter only lightly and add sugar slowly, beating no more than about three to five minutes. It is even better to mix ingredients together by hand using a wooden spoon. Letting cookie dough rest in the refrigerator for at least an hour before baking yields the best results.

When adding raisins, cranberries, or other fruits to a cake batter or cookie dough, dust the raisins with a little flour first. This helps keep them suspended in the batter or dough, rather than sinking to the bottom.

Folding

If the recipe directs you to fold ingredients such as egg whites, melted chocolate, nuts, and so on into a batter, gradually add the ingredient to the mixture and stir with a rubber spatula in a circular motion. Mix the ingredient while moving the spatula in the same direction, just until the ingredient is incorporated.

Melting Chocolate

There are several ways to melt chocolate, and the method is the same whether you are using dark chocolate, semisweet, or even white chocolate. The important thing is to not overheat chocolate, as it will turn grainy and lumpy. It's also critical that your implements and bowls be completely dry—even a few drops of water can cause your chocolate to seize. While you can melt it directly on the stovetop, it is a bit safer to use a double boiler or a microwave.

Melting chocolate directly on the stovetop: Chop the chocolate into even pieces and place them in a saucepan over very low heat. Stir constantly with a rubber spatula to prevent burning. As soon as the chocolate is completely melted and smooth, remove from heat. Allow to cool, then use.

If you want to melt chocolate with butter, place the two ingredients in the saucepan at the same time. Make sure the chocolate and the butter are cut into pieces and that the butter is room temperature. Follow the instructions above to melt.

Melting chocolate using a double boiler: If you do not have a double boiler, you can use any wide-mouth pot with a glass or metal bowl set snugly atop it. Bring a little water to a boil in the pot over medium heat; when the water is boiling, place the bowl over the mouth of the pot. Make sure that the water does not reach the bottom of the bowl. Put the pieces of chocolate into the bowl and stir gently until the chocolate is thoroughly melted and the mixture is uniform.

You can melt butter with chocolate in the same way, placing the two ingredients together and following the instructions above.

Melting chocolate in the microwave: Choose a microwave-safe bowl that stays relatively cool to the touch when heated in the microwave. Place the chopped chocolate in the bowl and heat at 50 percent power for thirty seconds. Stir gently with a rubber spatula and heat for another thirty seconds at half power. Continue heating for thirty seconds at a time, stirring each time, until the chocolate is smooth. The total amount of time required will vary depending upon the wattage of your microwave, the amount of chocolate, and the type of chocolate, but one ounce of chocolate will take approximately one minute to melt, while eight ounces will take approximately three minutes.

You can also melt butter with the chocolate using the same method.

Baking

Unless a recipe specifically says otherwise, always preheat your oven. Baking times assume that the oven is fully heated to the correct temperature before the cake or cookies are put into the oven. Actual oven temperatures may vary, and other factors such as brands of ingredients used and the surface of the pan may affect baking times. Always be sure to watch your cakes and cookies and test for doneness. A toothpick inserted into the center of a cake or cupcake should come out clean when the cake is done. The surface of a cake should spring back when touched with a finger. Cookies are typically done when they turn a golden color.

Unmolding a Baked Cake

Unless stated in the recipe to unmold the cake immediately allow the cake to cool, then slip a thin metal spatula between the side of the cake and the pan, running the blade around the edge to loosen the cake. Place a cardboard cake round (you can use parchment paper) on the cake and then place a plate over the paper round. Carefully flip the cake onto the plate. Gently pull the cake pan up and off of the cake. If the cake does not release easily, insert a knife between the top of the cake and the cake pan and press down lightly to break the seal between cake and pan.

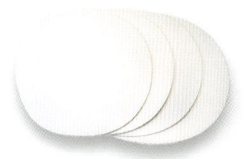

Cardboard cake round

Baking Pans

Prepare your pans before starting the recipe, and follow the directions for size and shape. Unless otherwise specified, baking pans should be greased and floured. For chocolate cakes, "flour" the pan with cocoa powder instead of flour. Many bakers like to use parchment paper, which guarantees that cookies slip right off the baking sheet and cakes drop easily out of the pan. Of course, parchment paper is not a viable solution if you are using a molded or fluted pan.

A wide array of decorative cupcake liners is now available, and these make cupcake baking much easier. While you can certainly grease and flour individual cupcake depressions, I encourage you to use pretty paper or foil liners, which ensure that your cupcakes come right out of the pan and also add decorative flair to your desserts.

Other Equipment

Following is the core team of kitchen tools that will serve you well for making the recipes in this book.

Heavy-duty stand mixer | Lazy Susan | Cutting board | Knives, serrated and butter

Strainer | Measuring spoons | Wire cooling rack | Cake pop sticks

Parchment paper | Rolling pin | Doilies | Stainless steel bowls

Cupcake papers * | Zester | Liquid measuring cups | Mixing bowls in graduated sizes & whisk | Dry measuring cup

Cookie cutters | Cake spreader | Cake stand | Cake server

Silicone/wooden spatula | Icing bags & tips | Pastry brush | Oven mitts

Icing Cakes

There are many ways to ice a cake, but one of the simplest methods yields a beautifully decorated cake and is easy to accomplish. First, turn your cake out so it rests on a paper round. This will allow you to move your cake once it's iced.

It's easiest to ice your cake if you set it on a cake stand so that it is closer to eye level. If you don't have a cake stand, simply invert a wide-bottomed mixing bowl and use it as a cake stand.

Begin frosting the cake by placing a large dollop of frosting on the top center of the cake. Spread from the center out toward the edges to cover the entire top of the cake. Be generous with frosting: you can always remove a bit if you've overdone it, but if you have too little, you may scrape up cake crumbs when you spread the frosting. Continue icing the edges and the sides, working from the top down. Then, holding the knife vertically, spread frosting around the sides, working from left to right to completely cover the cake.

Dipping your knife periodically in a glass of room-temperature water lets you achieve a smoother, more even effect.

Other Icing Techniques

You can create a more decorative effect with a pastry bag and decorative piping tips (if you don't have a pastry bag, you can use a heavy-duty freezer bag with a hole snipped from one corner). Fill the pastry bag with the frosting and, holding the decorating tip about one inch above the cake surface, gently squeeze the bag to push the frosting out of the tip. Various decorating tips will produce different effects, including thin or thick lines, swirls, and rosettes.

When using ganache, you can glaze the cake without using a knife or spatula. Place the ganache in a large measuring cup with a spout and drip it slowly over the center of the cake, letting the ganache run freely over the surface of the cake and down its sides until all of the cake is covered. Alternatively, you can smooth the ganache across the cake top using a large metal spatula or knife.

Glazes tend to be thinner when first made and harden as they dry. These can simply be drizzled or poured over the cake.

Frosting tips for Decorating

Cutting Cake

Use a large, sharp, warmed knife to cut cake. You can heat the knife by dipping it in a glass of very hot water and then wiping the blade before cutting each slice. Cut the cake in half, then cut in half again. Continue cutting all the way across the cake in even slices, depending on how many pieces you want.

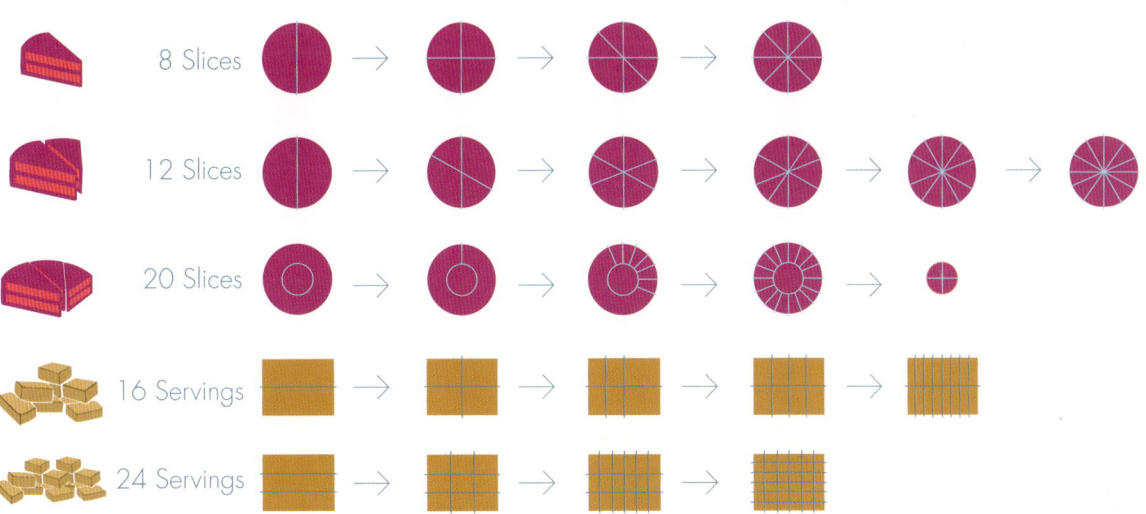

Icing Cupcakes

Decorating cupcakes is fun and it's a great activity to do with kids. Cupcakes can be frosted as cakes are, by placing a dollop of icing in the center of the cupcake and then spreading it to the edges.

For a more polished look, cupcakes can be iced using decorative tips and a pastry bag, opening up a world of creative possibilities. For an easy way to fill your icing bag, place the bag with the tip inserted (facing downward) into a wide-mouth cup or jar. Unfold the top of the bag outward over the rim of the cup. Use a silicone spatula to scoop the icing into the bag and use the rim of the cup to clean off the icing from the spatula, repeat to fill bag halfway. Lift the top of the bag from the container, gather and twist, and push the icing to the bottom to remove any air (two to three inches from the the top).

When frosting with a decorative tip, begin at the outside edge of the cupcake and work in a spiral pattern toward the center, as shown. For the best result, guide the tip steadily toward the center without stopping.

Coloring Icing

Especially if you like to decorate cakes and cupcakes and plan to do a lot of baking, consider buying concentrated icing color. These will give you intense colors without changing the consistency of your icing. For most colors, begin with white icing, but for brown or black colors begin with chocolate icing to avoid a change in flavor from large amounts of icing tint.

If you don't plan to decorate using colored icing very often, you may be satisfied with basic food coloring. These are available in most grocery stores, and come in red, green, yellow, and blue. Simply add drops to white icing until it is the color you desire. Be aware that it may be difficult to get bold or dark colors without adding enough liquid color to change the texture of the icing.

Stands

Stands are a fun and beautiful way to present your cupcakes to friends, family, and customers. Typically, a stand has one or more elevated levels that make it possible to show more of the cakes and cupcakes than if they were displayed on a simple plate. Stands are also good for preserving icing patterns, because the elevated design keeps a dessert from touching others and destroying the icing around its sides. Not only do stands make great centerpieces, they also elevate the mood of any party, inviting friends and family to admire and enjoy your delicious cupcakes.

Before you begin assembling your stands, clear your environment and make sure you have a flat space where you can work. Most stands are ready to assemble and require no outside materials, except your hands and perhaps clear tape for the truly cautious. To clean the stands after use, wipe off icing and crumbs with a damp sponge or cloth. Be careful not to use too much water, as that could damage the cardboard. Alternately, cover your stands with tin foil to keep them clean and reusable.

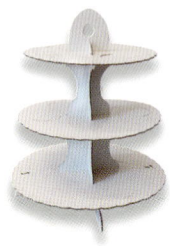

Cupcake stand

Assembling the Cupcake Stand

This display stand makes a great center piece. The two longer pieces will create the center "pedestal" for the stand. The pieces fit together with the help of pre-cut notches. Hold the shorter pedestal piece in your left hand, and the longer pedestal piece with the hole at the top in your right hand. Align the notch at the top of left (shorter) piece with the notch at the bottom of the right (taller) piece, so that they cross. Slide the longer piece down onto the shorter piece, until it reaches the bottom and forms an "X" shape.

Once the pedestal base of the stand is assembled, begin work on the "plate" levels. Lower the pre-cut disks onto the pedestal in order of largest to smallest, by aligning the pre-cut "X"-shaped notch in the disk with the top of the stand. Make sure each disk is in the appropriate place by moving them down until they reach their appropriate level and notch into place from underneath. This makes the stand a complete unit and allows you to pick it up and carry it around. If you want to give your stand more security, tape the disks to the base; note that this will make disassembly more difficult.

Cake pop stand

Assembling the Cake Pop Stand

This stand is best used during the preparation stage to catch icing drips. This stand is made of four pieces. The center pedestal consists of two small intersecting pieces. Hold the larger of these two pieces in your left hand, and the smaller piece in your right. Notch the bottom of the taller piece and the top of the smaller piece together, until they are fully integrated and make a complete base. One of the rectangle shelf pieces has a longer pre-cut notch; align this notch with the top of the stand base, then push down on the shelf piece until it reaches the bottom. Then do the same with the second rectangular shelf piece (with shorter pre-cut notches), pushing down until the notched space reaches its place in the middle of the stand.

Happy Baking!

With just a little effort you can create wonderful homemade desserts that your whole family will adore. From beginner-baker to seasoned practioner, the recipies within this book provide simple yet delicious solutions for every party need. From delicate cookies to lush chocolate cakes to festive cake pops, *Dessert Party* brings you dozens of crowd-pleasing treats designed to share with the ones you love.

Cakes

- Devil's Food Cake
- Chocolate Almond Mini Cakes
- Chocolate Chip Cake
- Vanilla Cake with Mocha Icing
- Golden Cake with Buttercream and Walnuts
- Sponge Cake with Strawberries and Whipped Cream
- Coconut Layer Cake
- German Chocolate Coconut Layer Cake
- Caramel Cake
- Carrot Cake with Cream Cheese Frosting
- Green Grapes Cake
- Apricot Upside Down Cake
- Apple Cake
- Orange–Nut Cake with Cointreau Syrup

DEVIL'S FOOD CAKE

This moist and airy layer cake will have chocoholics singing your praises. A decadent chocolate glaze is the perfect topping!

Preparation

1. Preheat oven to 350 degrees. Grease and flour with cocoa two 9-inch round cake pans.
2. Sift together the flour, baking soda, and salt, and set aside.
3. In a double boiler or in the microwave, melt chocolate until smooth, stirring constantly. Remove from heat and stir in hot coffee.
4. In a separate mixing bowl, using a mixer set to medium-high, beat butter until fluffy. Add sugar and continue beating. Add eggs one at a time, continuing to beat.
5. Stir melted chocolate/coffee into the butter, sugar, and eggs mixture.
6. Stir in sifted dry ingredients, a little at a time, alternating with buttermilk and vanilla.
7. Pour batter into prepared pans and bake for 30 minutes or until toothpick inserted into center comes out clean.
8. Allow to cool in pans 10 minutes before turning out on plates. Frost with Chocolate Glaze by pouring the glaze on the center of one cake and spreading it toward the edge. Top with the second layer and pour Chocolate Glaze over the center of the cake, letting it slowly drip down the sides.

Ingredients

- 2¼ cups flour
- 1 teaspoon baking soda
- 1 teaspoon salt
- 3 ounces unsweetened chocolate
- ¾ cup dark hot coffee
- ½ cup (1 stick) butter, softened
- 1½ cups sugar
- 3 eggs
- ½ cup buttermilk
- 1 teaspoon vanilla extract
- Chocolate Glaze (recipe page 135)

Difficulty
Easy

Baking Time
35–40 minutes

Portion
12 pieces

CHOCOLATE ALMOND MINI CAKES

With their dark, dense texture, these elegant little cakes add a glorious finishing touch to a special dinner.

Preparation

1. Preheat oven to 350°F. Grease and flour with cocoa 4 or 5 individual-sized round pans; as an alternative, you can use a 10-inch bundt pan. Set aside.
2. Separate the eggs. Beat egg whites until foamy. Set aside.
3. In a large mixing bowl, beat the egg yolks. Add the sugar to the yolks and stir.
4. In a medium saucepan over low heat, melt the semisweet and the unsweetened chocolate together with the butter over low heat and checking constantly. Or you could use a double boiler— see page 13. Once melted, add the chocolate to sugar and egg yolks mixture, then add almond extract.
5. In a food processor, grind almonds to the consistency of a coarse powder. Add almonds, flour, and salt to egg yolk mixture. Add in the beaten egg whites.
6. Pour batter into prepared pan and bake for 30 to 40 minutes, until a toothpick inserted into the center of the cake comes out clean. Allow cake to cool for 10 to 15 minutes, then turn out onto a serving plate. Decorate the top with sifted confectioners' sugar or drizzle with Rich Caramel Sauce.

Ingredients

- 4 eggs
- 1 cup sugar
- 3 ounces semisweet chocolate
- 3 ounces unsweetened chocolate
- ¾ cup butter
- ½ teaspoon almond extract
- ½ cup almonds, ground
- ¼ cup flour, sifted
- ¼ teaspoon salt
- Rich Caramel Sauce, if desired (recipe page 129)

Difficulty
Easy

Preparation Time
30–40 minutes

Portion
5 mini cakes

27

CHOCOLATE CHIP CAKE

Everybody loves this flavorful, chocolate-studded cake. Make a birthday extra special or delight your kids with a delicious after-school treat.

Ingredients

- 4 eggs
- 2 cups flour
- 2 teaspoons baking powder
- ½ teaspoon cream of tartar
- 1 cup (2 sticks) butter
- ¾ cup sugar
- ½ cup milk
- 1 teaspoon vanilla
- 1 cup chocolate chips
- 1 cup chopped nuts, such as walnuts or almonds
- Creamy Chocolate Frosting (recipe page 130)

Preparation

1. Preheat oven to 325°F. Grease and flour a tube pan or two 9-inch cake pans.
2. Separate eggs. In another bowl, sift together the flour and baking powder.
3. In a separate mixing bowl, beat egg whites with cream of tartar until fluffy. Set aside.
4. Beat together butter and sugar until creamy. Add egg yolks, one by one, continuing to beat mixture.
5. Add sifted dry ingredients a little at a time to the butter, egg, and sugar mixture, alternating with milk and vanilla.
6. Using a rubber spatula, fold egg whites into the batter.
7. Fold in chocolate chips and ½ cup of the nuts.
8. Pour batter into prepared tube pan and bake for 45 to 50 minutes, or until a toothpick inserted comes out clean.
9. Allow cake to cool for 10 to 15 minutes. Remove from pan to a cake plate. When completely cool, frost the cake with Creamy Chocolate Frosting and sprinkle with remaining nuts. As an alternative, frost with Easy Buttercream Frosting (recipe page 121).

Difficulty
Easy

Baking Time
45–50 minutes

Portion
12 pieces

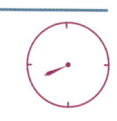

VANILLA CAKE WITH MOCHA ICING

In a simple but utterly enchanting combination, a traditional vanilla cake is frosted with coffee-infused icing and sprinkled with chopped walnuts.

Preparation

1. Preheat oven to 350°F. Grease two 9-inch cake pans or one tube pan.
2. Sift the flour, salt, and baking powder together and set aside.
3. In a separate mixing bowl, using an electric mixer set on medium–high, cream the butter with the sugar.
4. Add the eggs one by one and continue beating until creamy.
5. Slowly add the sifted dry ingredients a little at a time, alternating with milk and vanilla, and blend well.
6. Pour batter into prepared pan and bake for 40 minutes, or until toothpick inserted in center comes out clean.
7. Allow cake to cool for 10 minutes before removing to a cake plate. Once cake has cooled completely, frost with Mocha Icing and sprinkle with chopped nuts.

Ingredients

- 2 cups flour
- ¼ teaspoon salt
- 1 cup (2 sticks) butter
- 1 cup sugar
- 5 eggs
- ¾ cup milk
- 3 teaspoons baking powder
- 1 teaspoons vanilla
- Mocha Frosting (recipe page 127)

Difficulty
Easy

Baking Time
40 minutes

Portion
12 pieces

GOLDEN CAKE WITH BUTTERCREAM AND WALNUTS

Amazing for any occasion, this classic pound cake is rich and tasty. Eat it plain or spread the top with Easy Buttercream Frosting or one of the other delicious frostings.

Preparation

1. Preheat oven to 325°F. Grease and flour a 13-inch tube pan.
2. Sift together the flour and baking powder. Separate 5 eggs, reserving yolks for another use.
3. Beat 5 egg whites with an electric mixer on high until stiff.
4. In a separate mixing bowl, cream together the butter and sugar. Once the mixture is creamy, add 7 whole eggs one by one, beating well.
5. Slowly add sifted dry ingredients, alternating with the milk and vanilla.
6. Mix in the 5 beaten egg whites using a in a rolling motion wooden spoon in a rolling motion.
7. Put batter into the prepared pan and bake for 1 hour or until a toothpick inserted in the center comes out clean.
8. Allow to cool for 15 to 20 minutes, then turn out onto a plate.
9. When cake is completely cool, frost with Easy Buttercream Frosting and press walnuts into the top and sides.

Ingredients

4	cups flour
4	teaspoons of baking powder
12	eggs
2	cups (4 sticks) butter, softened
2	cups sugar
1	cup milk
1	teaspoon vanilla extract
	Easy Buttercream Frosting (recipe page 121)
1	cup of chopped walnuts

Difficulty
Easy

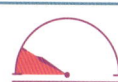

Preparation Time
1 hour

Portion
12–16 pieces

SPONGE CAKE WITH STRAWBERRIES AND WHIPPED CREAM

An airy sponge cake is slathered with whipped cream and decked with halved strawberries for a twist on strawberry shortcake—perfect with afternoon tea.

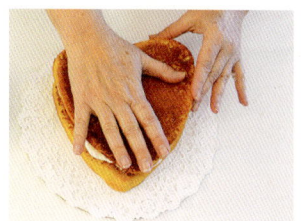   

Preparation

1. Preheat oven to 325°F. Grease two 9-inch cake pans.
2. Sift flour and set aside.
3. In a separate mixing bowl, beat the eggs with an electric mixer set to medium–high until thick. Add sugar little by little, continuing to beat.
4. Add sifted flour to egg and sugar mixture, alternating with water and vanilla.
5. Pour batter into prepared cake pans and bake 30 minutes or until toothpick inserted in the center comes out clean. Allow cakes to cool in pan for 10 minutes then remove to cake plates.
6. Cover bottom layer of cake with Whipped Cream and sprinkle with chopped strawberries. Top with second cake. Then cover top and sides of cake with Whipped Cream and decorate with the halved strawberries.

Ingredients

- 6 eggs
- 1 cup sugar
- cups flour
- ¼ cup cold water
- 1 teaspoon vanilla extract
- Whipped Cream (recipe page 119)
- 1 cup fresh strawberries, half chopped and half halved

Difficulty
Easy to intermediate

Baking Time
30 minutes

Portion
8 pieces
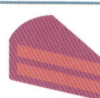

33

COCONUT LAYER CAKE

One of my mom's favorite recipes, this classic layer cake reminds me of a snow-covered landscape—a delicious one!

Preparation

1. Preheat oven to 350°F. Grease two 9-inch round cake pans and set aside.
2. In a large bowl, sift together flour, baking powder, and salt. Set aside.
3. Separate the eggs. In large mixing bowl, beat egg whites until stiff, about 5 minutes. Set aside.
4. In your largest bowl, using an electric mixer on low speed, beat the butter for 2 to 3 minutes. Add the sugar and continue beating for 5 minutes, until light and fluffy.
5. Add in one egg yolk at a time and continue beating until creamy, 2 or 3 more minutes. (Two egg yolks are not used).
6. Add the sifted dry ingredients gradually, alternating with the milk and vanilla, beating on low speed. Fold in egg whites using a spatula.
7. Pour batter into prepared pans and bake for 30 to 35 minutes, until a toothpick inserted into the center comes out clean.
8. Let cool in the pans on wire racks for 10 minutes. Place the wire rack on top of the pan, and flip over to release the cakes. Let cakes continue cooling directly on the wire racks.
9. Place one layer on a serving plate and spread 3 to 4 tablespoons of Vanilla Filling Cream over the top until it is evenly covered, using additional cream if necessary, until the layer is completely covered. Place the second layer on top of the first and frost the top and sides of the cake with Easy Buttercream Frosting. Sprinkle coconut evenly over the top of the cake and press coconut into the sides, making sure it is evenly distributed. Set cake in a cool room.

Ingredients

- 3 cups flour
- 4 teaspoons baking powder
- ¼ teaspoon salt
- 6 egg whites
- 1 cup butter (2 sticks)
- 2 cups sugar
- 4 egg yolks
- 1¾ cups milk
- 1 teaspoons vanilla extract
- 3-4 tablespoons *Vanilla Filling Cream (recipe page 120)*
- 1 cup flaked coconut
- *Easy Buttercream Frosting (recipe page 121)*

Difficulty
Easy to intermediate

Baking Time
30–35 minutes

Portion
12–16 pieces

GERMAN CHOCOLATE COCONUT LAYER CAKE

This three-layer cake is a made with sweet baking chocolate in the traditional way. Adding the signature coconut and pecan-studded German Chocolate Frosting turns this lush cake into a sweet and sticky treat.

Preparation

1. Preheat oven to 350°F.
2. Grease and flour three 9-inch round pans. Cut three round pieces of parchment paper and place them in the bottom of each pan, then set aside.
3. Sift together the flour, baking powder, and salt, then set aside.
4. Melt the chocolate and the milk together over low heat, stirring constantly. Set aside. In a separate mixing bowl, using an electric mixer set on medium, cream the butter. Add sugar to the butter gradually, beating well. Once butter and sugar are well mixed, add eggs one by one and mix well.
5. Add sifted dry ingredients to the butter mixture, then add milk with chocolate and mix until well combined.
6. Fill the prepared pans with the batter and bake for 30 minutes or until a toothpick comes out clean. Cool for 10 minutes before turning cakes out onto a plate.
7. Use German Chocolate Frosting to fill between layers and frost the top of the cake.

Ingredients

- 2 cups flour
- 2 teaspoons baking powder
- ¼ teaspoon salt
- 2 ounces sweet chocolate
- 1 cup of milk
- ½ pound butter (2 sticks)
- 1 cup sugar
- 3 eggs
- German Chocolate Frosting (page 134)

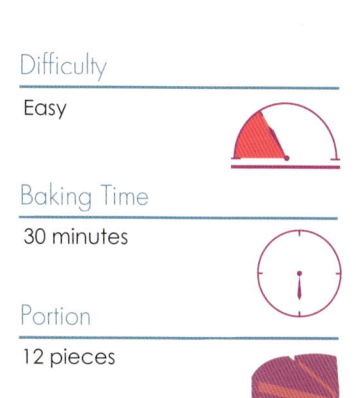

Difficulty
Easy

Baking Time
30 minutes

Portion
12 pieces

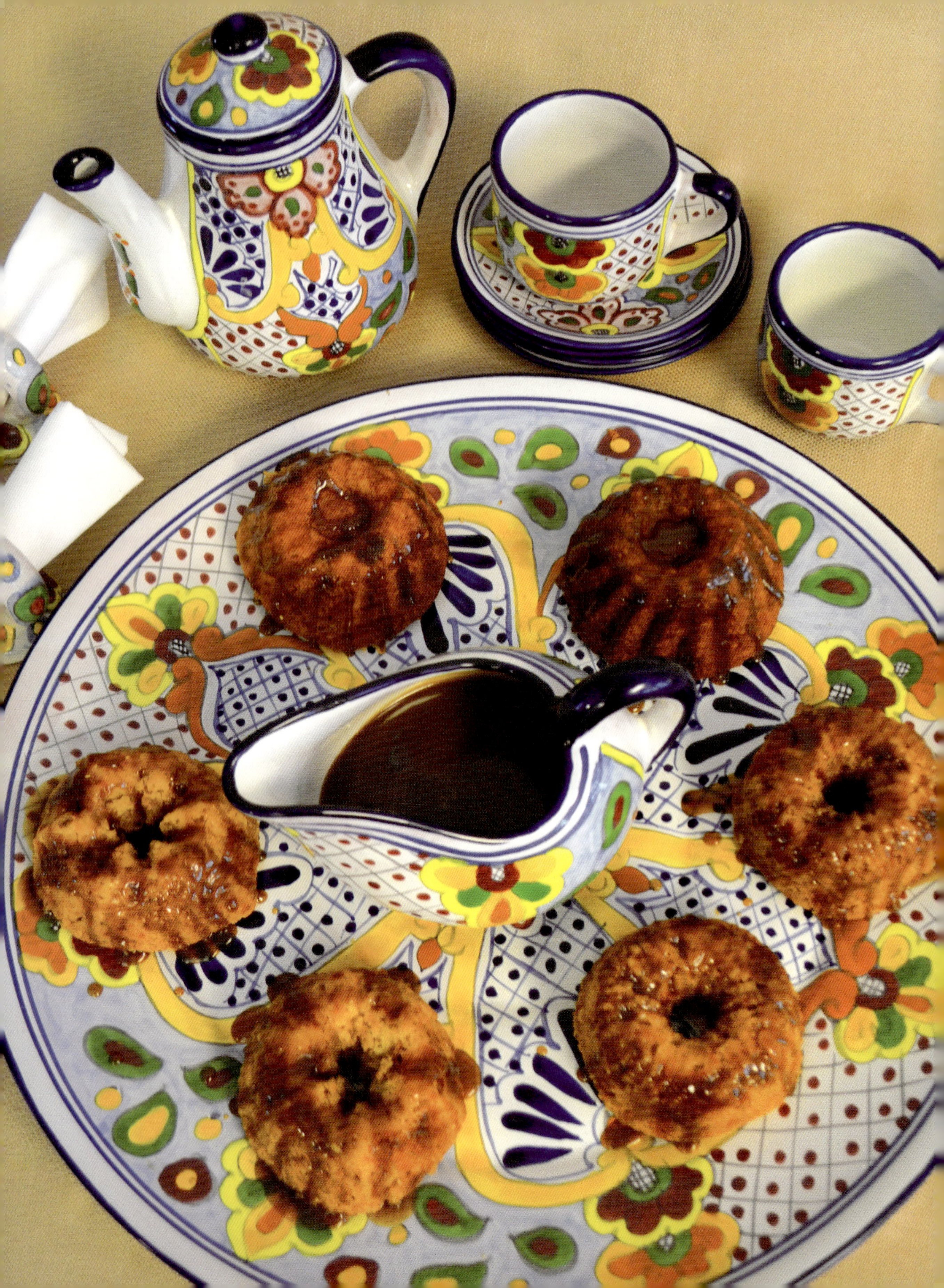

CARAMEL CAKE

Elegant and delicious, this cake is a little bit of heaven! Rich caramel sauce flavors the cake and serves as a glaze as well.

Preparation

1. Preheat oven to 325°F. Grease and flour two 9-inch cake pans or six mini bundt pans.
2. Make Rich Caramel Sauce, on page 129, up to step 3 and set aside.
3. Sift together flour with salt and baking powder. Set aside.
4. In a separate mixing bowl, cream butter with an electric mixer, adding white and brown sugars gradually. Add the eggs one by one. Stir in vanilla.
5. Combine ⅓ cup Caramel (from step 2 above) and ⅔ cup water to make 1 cup of liquid.
6. Add Caramel Sauce and sifted dry ingredients to butter and sugar mixture alternately while beating well.
7. Pour batter evenly into the two cake pans and bake 35 to 40 minutes or until a toothpick inserted into the center comes out clean.
8. Allow cake to cool in pans for 10 minutes then turn out onto plates. Finish preparing the Rich Caramel Sauce as indicated in recipe and pour over bottom layer and sprinkle with nuts, if desired. Top with second layer and pour Caramel Sauce over cake. Sprinkle with nuts again, if desired.

Ingredients

Rich Caramel Sauce (recipe page 129)
- 2⅓ cups flour
- ⅓ teaspoon salt
- 2½ teaspoons baking powder
- ½ cup butter
- ¾ cup sugar
- ½ cup brown sugar
- 3 eggs
- 1 teaspoon vanilla extract
- ⅔ cup water
- 1 cup walnuts or pecans (optional)

Difficulty
Intermediate

Baking Time
35–40 minutes

Portion
12 pieces or 6 mini bundt cakes

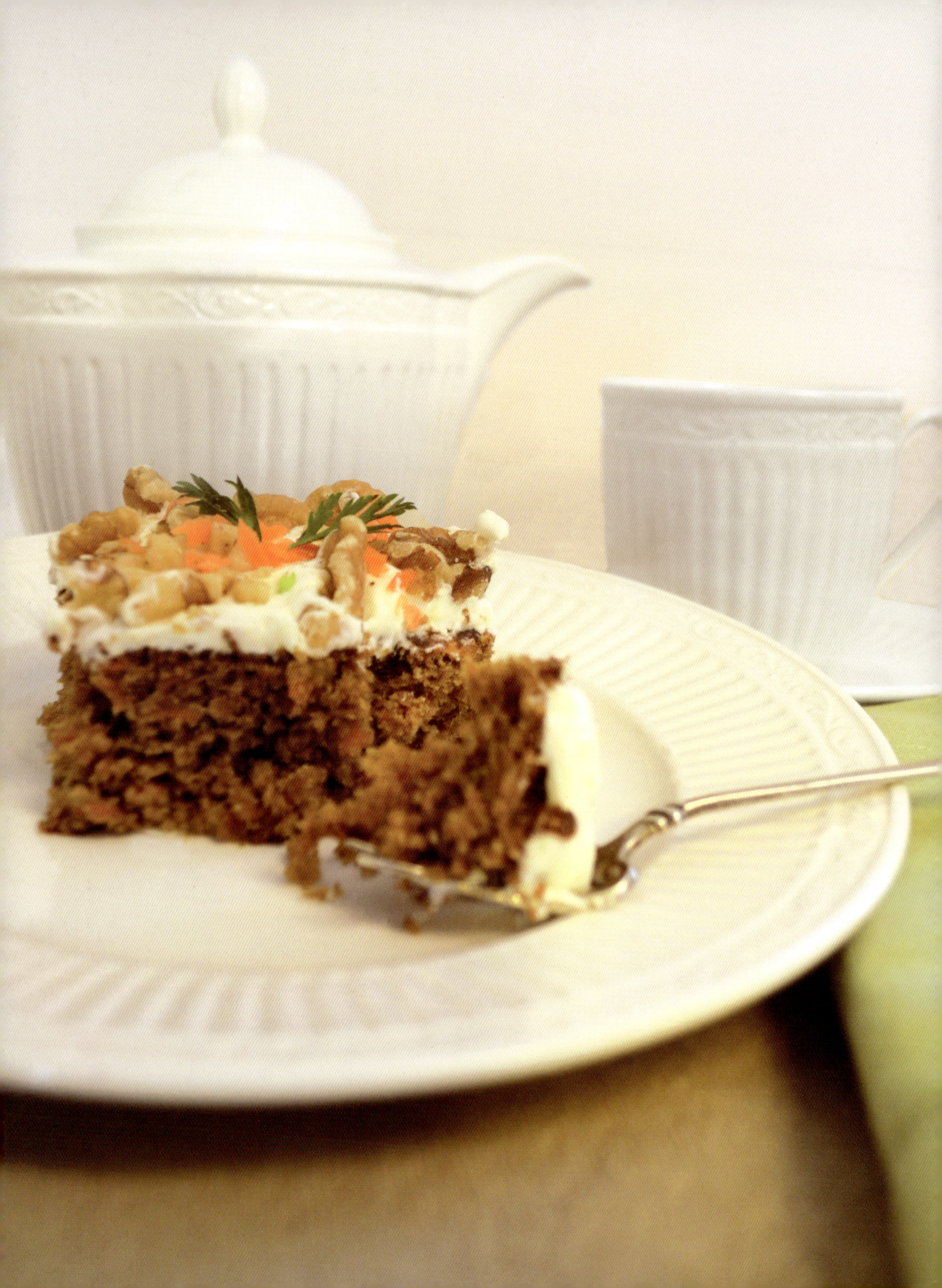

CARROT CAKE WITH CREAM CHEESE FROSTING

Perfect for large gatherings, this classic carrot cake's single layer makes it easy to serve. The silky cream cheese frosting always gets a thumbs-up from my son-in-law.

Preparation

1. Preheat oven to 350°F. Grease a 13-by-9-inch pan and set aside.
2. Sift together the flour, baking powder, baking soda, cinnamon, and nutmeg. Set aside.
3. In a separate mixing bowl, using an electric mixer on low, beat the butter until light and fluffy (3 minutes), then add the brown sugar and beat 2 more minutes. Add the eggs one at a time and continue mixing.
4. Add the sifted dry ingredients to the wet ingredients slowly, alternating with the milk, until all has been incorporated.
5. Fold in the carrots, then the raisins and walnuts.
6. Pour batter into prepared cake pan. Bake for 30 to 40 minutes, or until toothpick inserted in center comes out clean.
7. When cake is completely cool, spread Cream Cheese Frosting on top and sides of cake, and decorate with carrot shavings and walnuts.

Ingredients

- 1¼ cups flour
- 2 teaspoons baking powder
- ½ teaspoon baking soda
- 1 teaspoon cinnamon
- 1 teaspoon nutmeg
- 1½ cup butter (1 stick)
- 1½ cups brown sugar
- 2 eggs
- ½ cup milk
- 1½ cups fresh carrots, shredded, plus extra for decoration
- ½ cup raisins
- ¾ cup walnuts, chopped, plus extra for sprinkling
- Cream cheese Frosting (recipe page 126)

Difficulty
Easy to intermediate

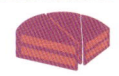

Baking Time
30-40 minutes

Portion
24 pieces

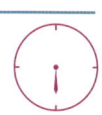

41

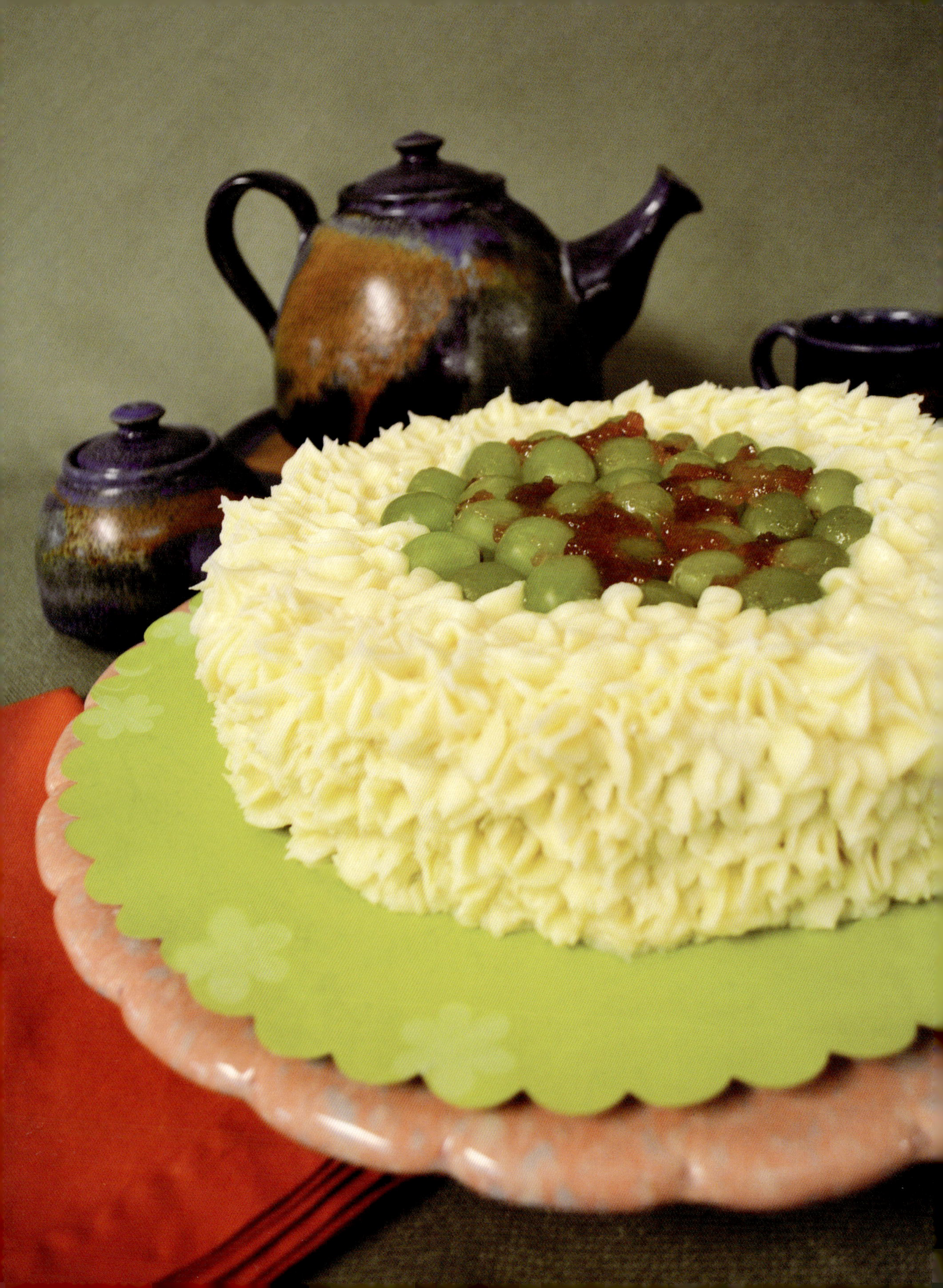

GREEN GRAPES CAKE

Wonderful presentation and an exquisite flavor with notes of citrus make this special cake stand out in a crowd.

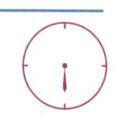

Preparation

1. Preheat oven to 350°F. Grease two 9-inch round cake pans. Sift the flour and baking powder. Set aside.
2. In a separate mixing bowl, using an electric mixer, beat the eggs until foamy. Add sugar gradually, continuing to beat.
3. Slowly add sifted dry ingredients to the egg and sugar mixture, alternating with the cold water and vanilla.
4. Divide batter evenly into the prepared cake pans.
5. Bake for 30 minutes. Cool slightly, then remove cake from pans.
6. While cake is still warm, spoon half the liqueur over bottom layer, then cover with jelly. Cover with top cake layer, and spoon liqueur over top.
7. When the cake has cooled, arrange green grapes in the center of cake and brush the grapes with apricot jelly.
8. Pipe with Easy Buttercream Frosting.

Ingredients

- 2 cups flour
- 2 teaspoons baking powder
- 6 eggs
- 1¼ cups sugar
- 1 cup cold water
- 1 teaspoon vanilla extract
- 1 pound fresh green grapes
- 1½ ounces orange-flavored liqueur
- 1 cup apricot jelly
- *Easy Buttercream Frosting (recipe page 121)*

Difficulty
Easy

Baking Time
30 minutes

Portion
12 pieces

APRICOT UPSIDE-DOWN CAKE

This modern twist on the pineapple upside-down cake is the ideal summer dessert—fresh, seasonal, and fun to make!

Preparation

1. Preheat oven to 350°F.
2. Sift together the flour, baking powder, and salt and set aside.
3. Melt butter in a small saucepan, then pour into a 9 ½-inch glass pie plate. Sprinkle brown sugar evenly over the butter. Place apricots in the pie plate cut side down, with one in the center and the others surrounding it to form a flower shape.
4. In a mixing bowl, beat eggs with an electric mixer set on low speed until they are fluffy. Add white sugar and continue beating until well combined.
5. Stir in sifted dry ingredients.
6. Add water and vanilla and mix well.
7. Drop batter gently and spread over pie plate, being careful not to disturb the arrangement of the apricots. Bake for 40 to 45 minutes, until the cake is golden and a toothpick inserted into the middle comes out clean.
8. Cool for 10 minutes, then invert the cake onto a large serving plate.

Ingredients

- 1 cup flour
- ⅓ teaspoon baking powder
- ¼ teaspoon salt
- ½ cup (1 stick) butter
- 1 cup brown sugar
- 6 fresh apricots, halved and pitted
- 4 eggs
- ⅔ cup granulated white sugar
- 6 tablespoons cold water
- 1 teaspoon vanilla

Difficulty
Intermediate

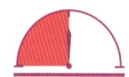

Preparation Time
40–45 minutes

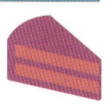

Portion
8 pieces

45

APPLE CAKE

This moist cake is redolent with fresh, sweet apples. It's my friend, Patricia Jimenez's recipe—she served it warm with a scoop of vanilla ice cream at my daughter's bridal shower.

Preparation

1. Preheat oven to 350°F. Grease and flour a 10-inch tube pan or six small (5-inch) pans.
2. Sift together the flour, cinnamon, nutmeg, baking soda, and salt.
3. In a separate bowl, using an electric mixer, cream the butter with the white sugar and brown sugar for about 5 minutes, until light and airy. Add the eggs one at a time, mixing thoroughly into the butter and sugar. Add the vanilla.
4. Add the dry ingredients to the wet ingredients and mix together until just blended; do not overmix.
5. Gently fold in the apples and walnuts.
6. Fill the prepared pan with the batter and bake for 50 to 60 minutes, until a toothpick inserted into the center comes out clean. When the cake has cooled, remove it to a cake plate and top with glaze.

Ingredients

- 3 cups flour
- 2 teaspoons cinnamon
- ½ teaspoon nutmeg
- 1 teaspoon baking soda
- ¼ teaspoon salt
- 1½ cups butter (3 sticks)
- 1½ cups sugar
- ½ cup brown sugar
- 3 eggs
- 2 teaspoons vanilla extract
- 4 cups peeled and chopped apples, about 3 to 5 medium
- 1 cup walnuts, chopped

Vanilla Glaze (recpie page 117)

Difficulty
Easy to intermediate

Baking Time
50–60 minutes

Portion
12 pieces

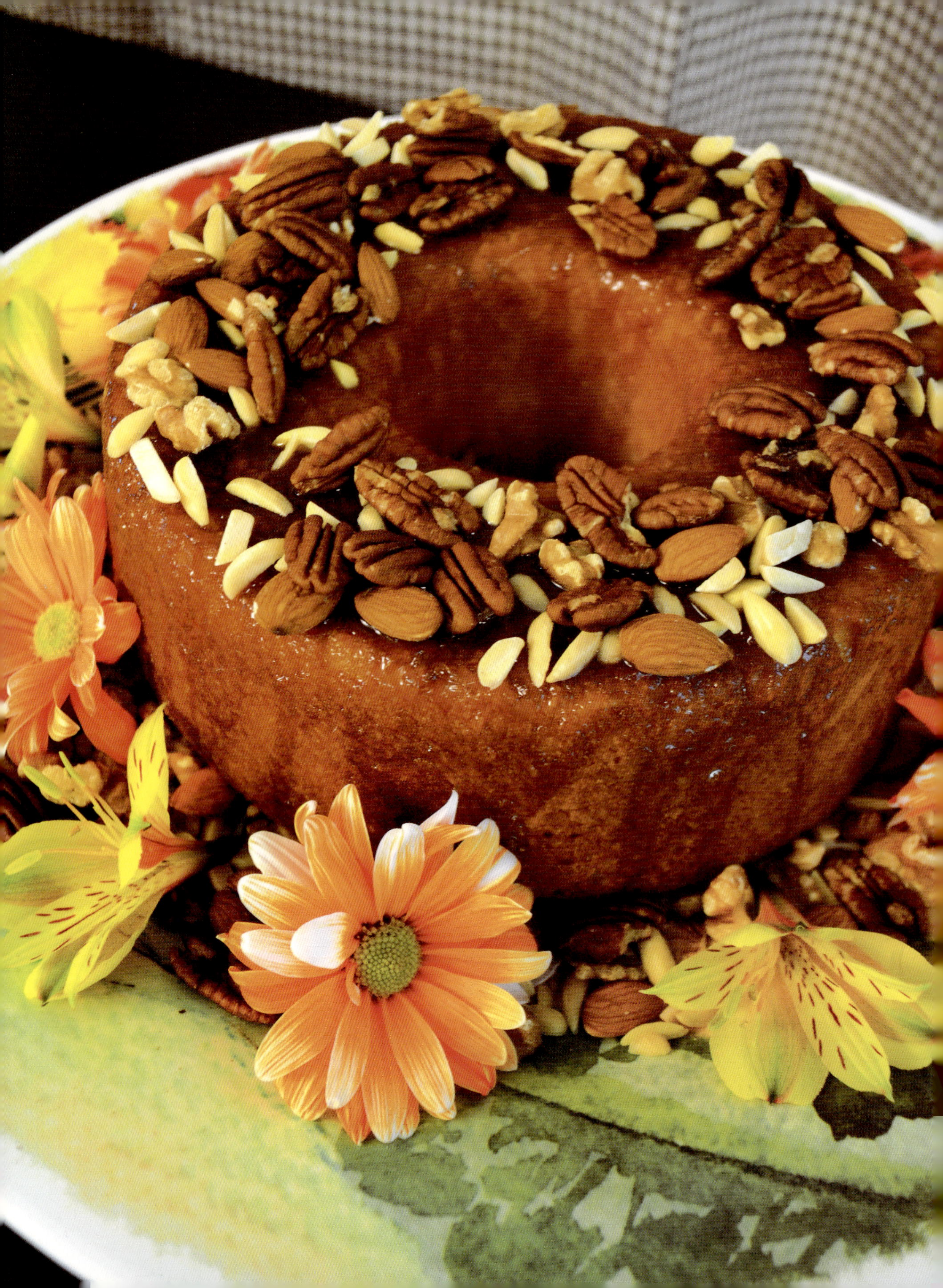

ORANGE-NUT CAKE WITH COINTREAU SYRUP

Orange-flavored liqueur and fresh orange juice pair with chopped nuts and raisins for a simple but delicious treat.

Preparation

1. Preheat oven to 325°F. Grease and flour a tube pan.
2. Separate the eggs. With an electric mixer, beat the egg whites only until stiff.
3. Sift together flour, baking powder, and salt and set aside.
4. In a separate mixing bowl, with an electric mixer set on medium–high, beat butter with sugar until it is creamy. Add the egg yolks one by one.
5. Slowly add sifted dry ingredients to the butter, sugar, and eggs, alternating with orange juice. Mix well. Add in the egg whites and beat until mixed.
6. Bake for 50 to 60 minutes or until a toothpick inserted in the center comes out clean.
7. Allow to cool in pan for 20 minutes then slide cake from pan. If desired, fill hollow in center of cake with mixed nuts and raisins. Pour Cointreau Syrup over the cake while it is still warm.

Ingredients

- 4 eggs
- 2 cups flour
- 2½ teaspoons of baking powder
- 1 pinch salt
- 1 cup (2 sticks) butter, softened
- 1 cup sugar
- 1 teaspoon vanilla extract
- ½ cup orange juice
- Cointreau Syrup (recipe page 116)
- ¼ cup each chopped walnuts, almonds, hazelnuts, and cashews (optional)
- ¼ cup raisins (optional)

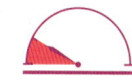

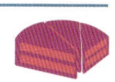

Difficulty
Easy

Baking Time
50–60 minutes

Portion
16 pieces

Cupcakes

- Super-Rich Chocolate Cupcakes -
- Chocolate–Orange Cupcakes -
- Cupcakes with Sour Cream and Raisins -
- Red Velvet Cupcakes -
- Vanilla Cupcakes -
- Chai Cupcakes -

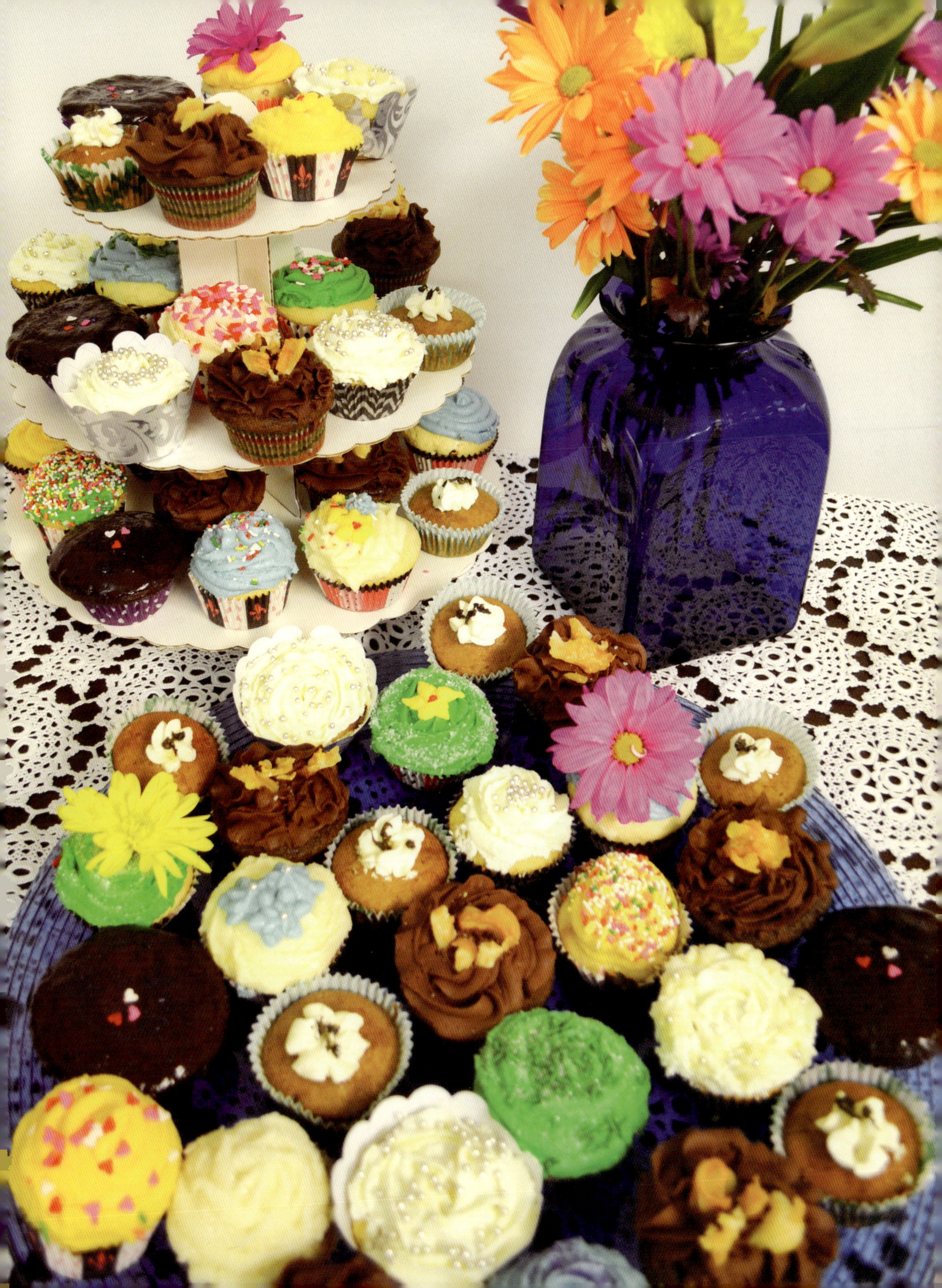

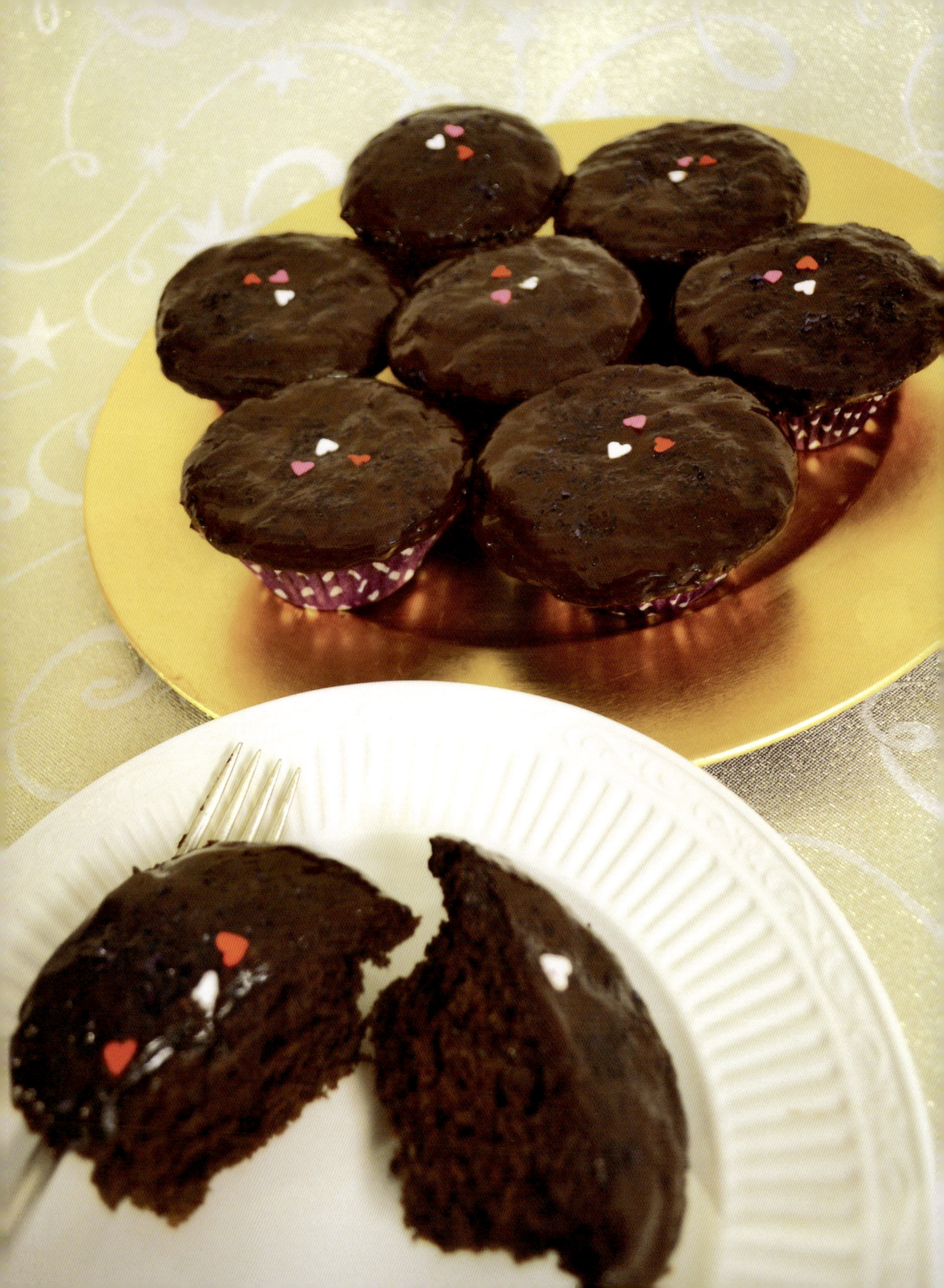

SUPER-RICH CHOCOLATE CUPCAKES

Cocoa gives these little gems their lush, chocolate flavor. Ganache spread on top makes these cupcakes truly "super rich"!

Preparation

1. Preheat oven to 350°F. Line a cupcake tin with 12 foil or paper liners.
2. Sift together the flour, cocoa, baking powder, and salt, and set aside.
3. In a separate bowl, cream together the butter, white sugar, and brown sugar. Add the eggs one by one. Add vanilla.
4. Add the dry ingredients slowly to the mixing bowl, alternating with milk, until combined.
5. Dissolve baking soda into the boiling water and add to batter, mixing until blended.
6. Fill the cupcake liners with batter about two-thirds full. Bake for 20 minutes or until a toothpick inserted comes out clean.
7. Cool for five minutes in tin, then turn out on wire racks to cool completely. When cupcakes have cooled completely, spread with *Ganache*.

Ingredients

- 2 cups flour
- ½ cup of cocoa
- 2 teaspoons baking powder
- ½ teaspoon salt
- ½ cup butter (1 stick), softened
- 1 cup granulated white sugar
- ½ cup brown sugar
- 2 eggs
- 1 teaspoon vanilla extract
- ½ cup milk
- 1 cup boiling water
- 1 teaspoon baking soda
- *Ganache* (recipe page 133)

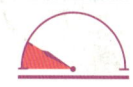

Difficulty
Easy

Baking Time
20 minutes

Portion
12 cupcakes

ORANGE-CHOCOLATE CUPCAKES

Zesty orange is a delightful complement for these velvety chocolate cakes, which are topped with Creamy Chocolate Frosting and garnished with candied orange peel for a sophisticated presentation.

Preparation

1. Preheat oven to 350°F. Line a muffin tin with 12 paper or foil cupcake liners.
2. In a small saucepan over low heat, melt the butter and cocoa powder together. Set aside.
3. In a large bowl, sift together flour, baking powder and salt. Add the grated orange peel to the sifted dry ingredients. Set aside.
4. In a separate bowl, using an electric mixer set on low speed, beat the eggs until they rise and get thick. Add the white and brown sugars and mix well.
5. Continuing on low speed, add the melted butter and cocoa, plus the milk and orange extract, to the egg and sugar mixture.
6. Add the sifted dry ingredients, continuing to mix just until blended. Dissolve baking soda into the hot water and mix into batter.
7. Spoon the batter into prepared cupcake papers, filling each three-quarters full. Bake for 18 to 20 minutes, until a toothpick inserted into the middle comes out clean.
8. Cool on wire rack in pans until completely cooled.
9. Spread or pipe Creamy Chocolate Frosting. Decorate tops with candied orange peel.

Ingredients

- ¼ cup butter (½ stick)
- 3 tablespoons cocoa powder
- 1¼ cups flour
- ½ teaspoon baking powder
- ¼ teaspoon salt
- ¼ cup finely grated orange peel
- 2 eggs
- ½ cup sugar
- ¼ cup brown sugar
- ½ cup milk
- ½ teaspoon orange extract
- ½ teaspoon baking soda
- ¼ cup hot water
- *Creamy Chocolate Frosting (recipe page 130)*
- Candied orange peel, for garnish

Difficulty
Intermediate

Preparation Time
20 minutes

Portion
12 cupcakes

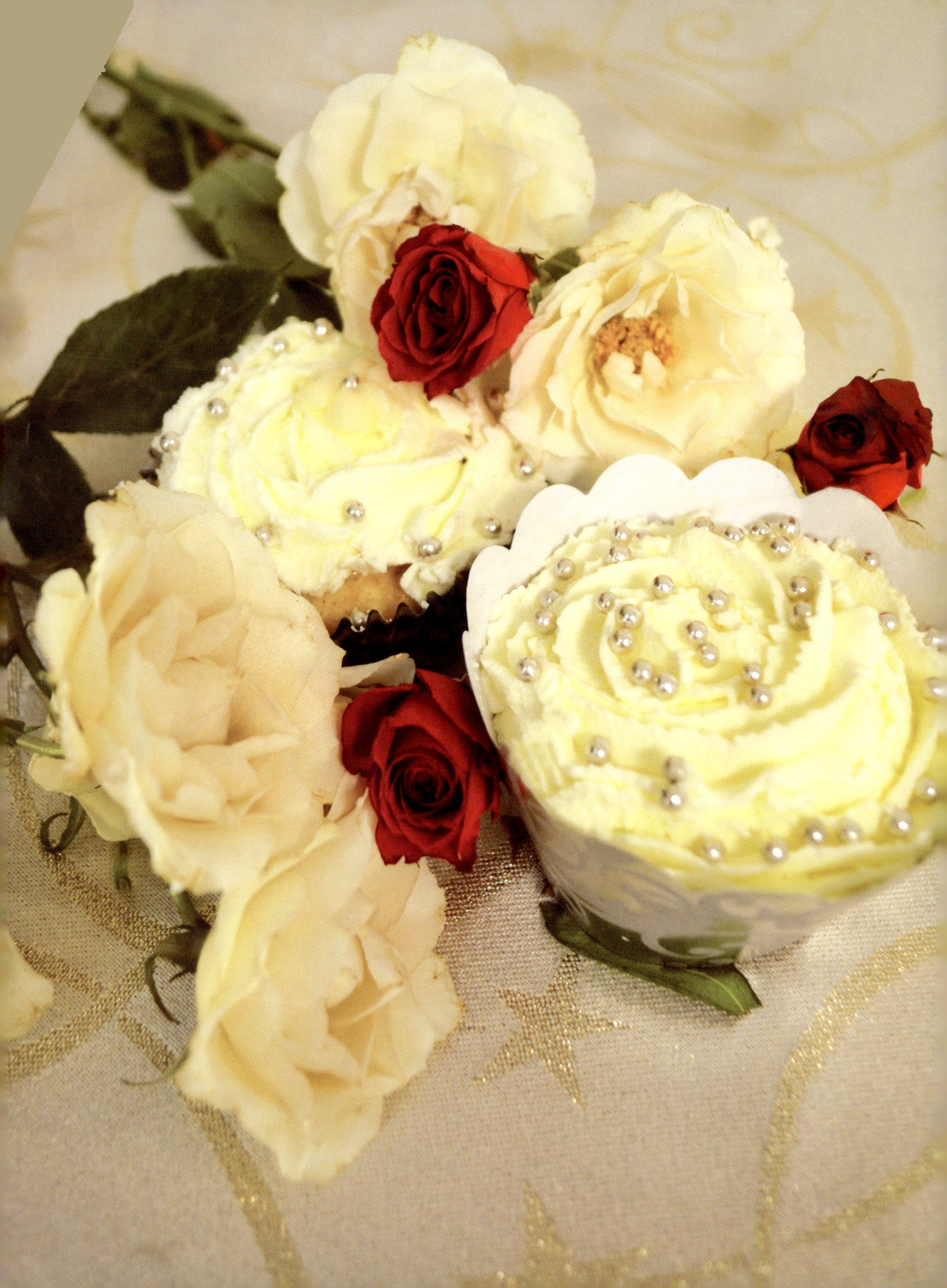

CUPCAKES WITH SOUR CREAM AND RAISINS

Sour cream gives these cupcakes a soft and tender texture that's hard to match. And they're a terrific stage for all your decorating whims!

Preparation

1. Preheat oven to 350°F. Line 12 muffin cups with paper or foil liners and set aside.
2. Beat eggs until thick and foamy. Add sugar and continue beating until well combined.
3. In a separate mixing bowl, sift together flour and baking powder. Add to egg and sugar mixture and mix until combined.
4. Add orange juice, then stir in sour cream. Fold in raisins.
5. Pour batter into prepared baking cups and bake for 35 to 40 minutes or until cupcakes spring back to the touch. Let cupcakes cool in tins about 5 minutes, then turn them out onto wire racks to cool completely.
6. Frost with Easy Buttercream Frosting. Alternatively, ice with Cream Cheese Frosting (recipe page 121) or the icing of your choice.

Ingredients

- 3 eggs
- 1½ cups sugar
- 2½ cups flour
- 1½ teaspoon baking powder
- 1 teaspoon fresh orange juice
- 1½ cups sour cream
- ½ cup raisins
- *Easy Buttercream Frosting (recipe page 121)*

Difficulty
Easy

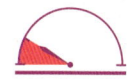

Preparation Time
35–40 minutes

Portion
12 cupcakes

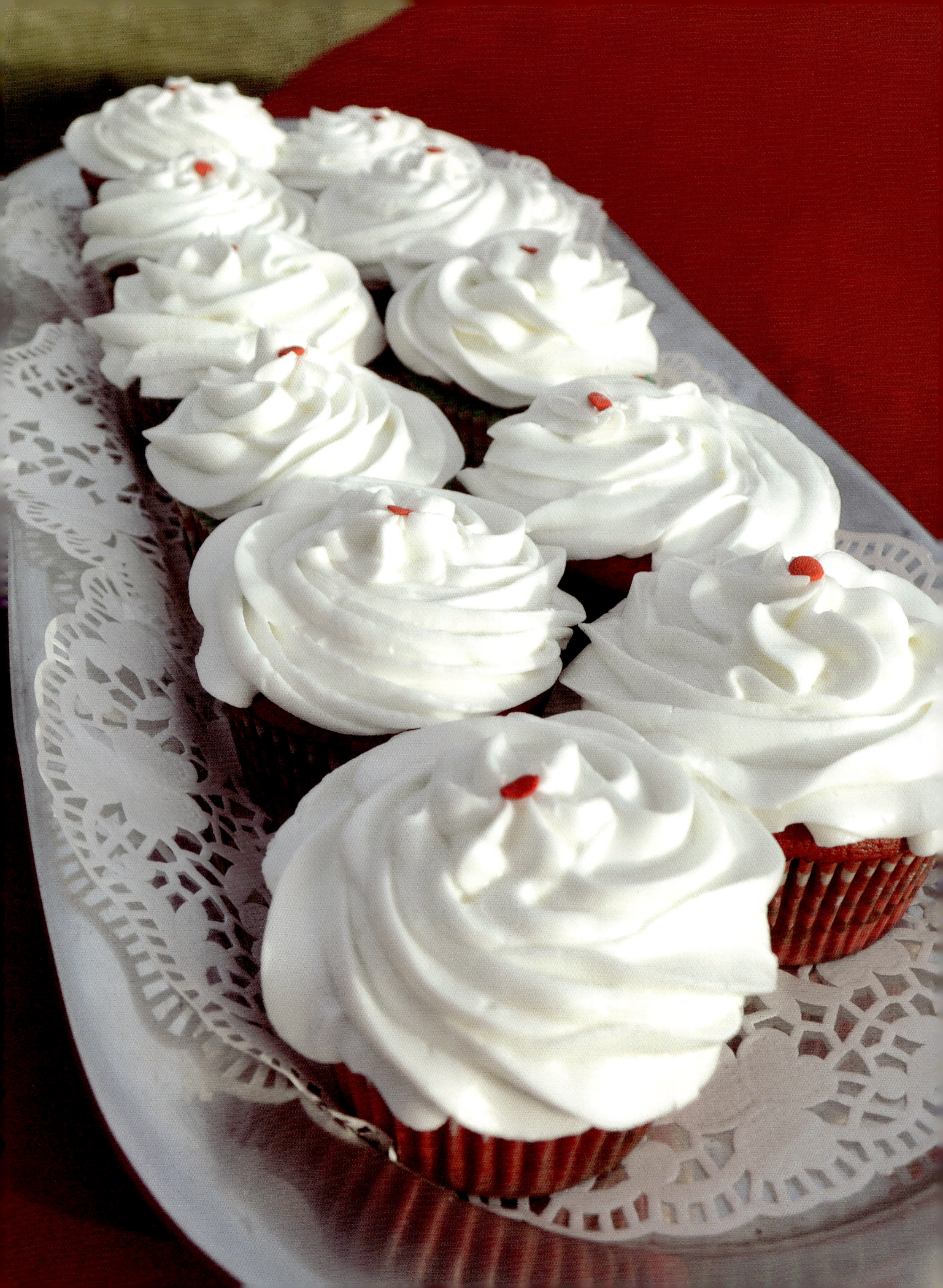

RED VELVET CUPCAKES

With their signature color and chocolate essence, these cupcakes are and of the moment. Perfect any time of year, they're especially delightful as a Valentine surprise.

Preparation

1. Preheat oven to 350°F. Line 12 muffin cups with paper or foil liners and set aside.
2. Dissolve baking soda in the water. In a separate bowl, sift together flour and salt, and set aside.
3. Melt butter over medium-low heat, and stir in cocoa powder, being careful not to burn the mixture.
4. In a separate mixing bowl, beat eggs with an electric mixer set on low until fluffy and lighter in color.
5. Add chocolate mix, then natural red food coloring, and mix well.
6. Stir in sifted dry ingredients until they are incorporated.
7. Stir in buttermilk and vanilla, then add dissolved baking soda-water mixture, and stir until combined.
8. Fill prepared cups about three-quarters full and bake, rotating pans once, for 20 to 25 minutes, or until cupcakes spring back to the touch. Let cupcakes cool in tins about 5 minutes, then turn them out onto wire racks to cool completely.
9. Decorate with Easy Buttercream Frosting or the frosting of your choice.

Ingredients

- 1 teaspoon baking soda
- 2 teaspoons water
- 2½ cups flour
- 1 teaspoon salt
- ½ cup (1 stick) butter
- 3 tablespoons unsweetened cocoa powder (or 3 ounces unsweetened chocolate)
- 2 eggs
- 12 drops natural red food coloring
- 1 cup buttermilk
- 1 teaspoon vanilla
- *Easy Buttercream Frosting (recipe page 121)*

Difficulty
Easy

Baking Time
20–25 minutes

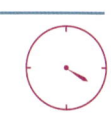

Portion
12 cupcakes

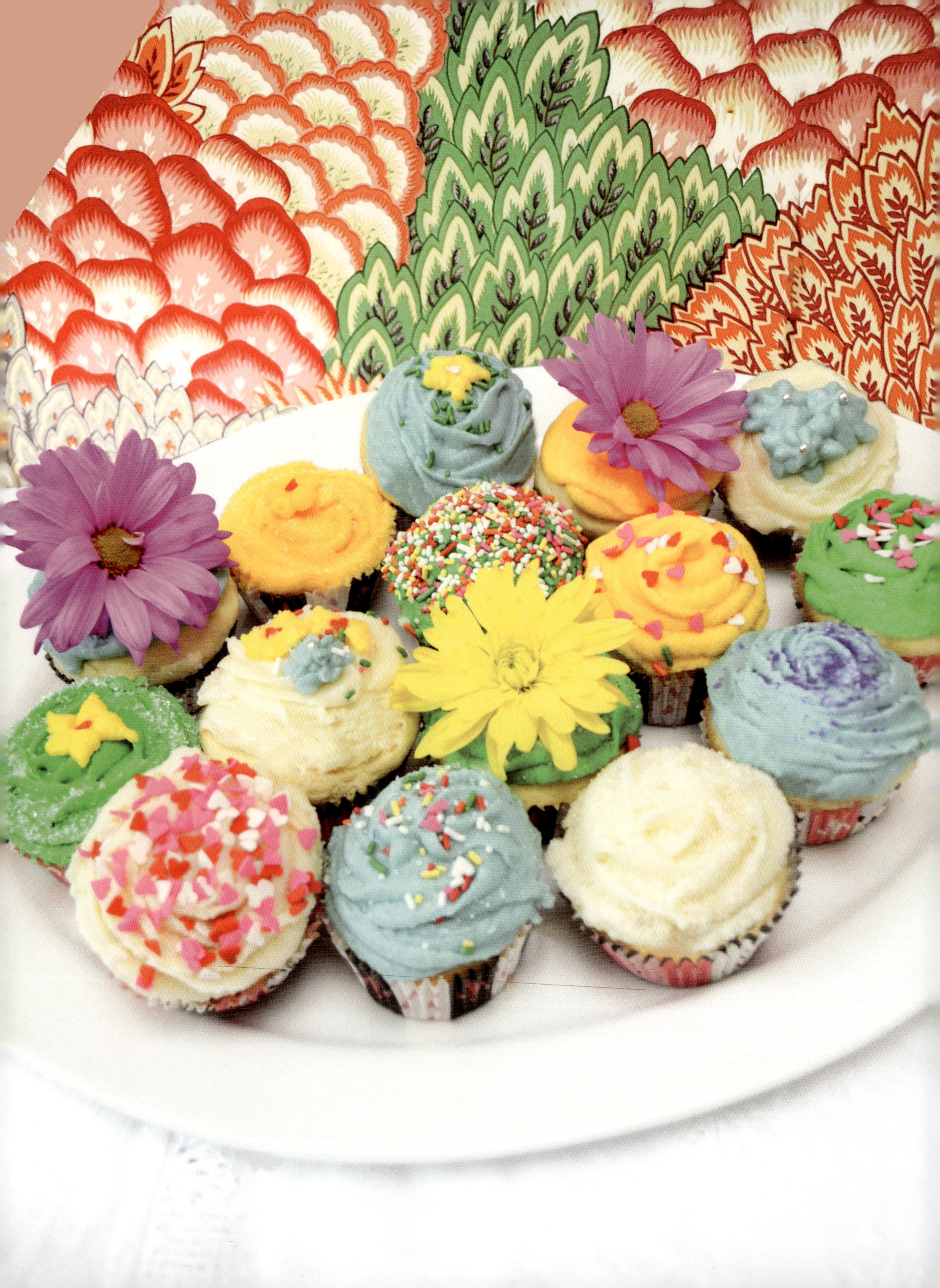

VANILLA CUPCAKES

These simple cupcakes are the ideal platform for the frostings and embellishments of your choice. Their subtle vanilla flavor complements whatever wild combinations you can dream up!

Preparation

1. Preheat oven to 350°F. Line 12 muffin cups with paper or foil liners and set aside.
2. Sift together the flour, baking powder, and salt, and set aside.
3. Cream the butter with an electric mixer set on medium-low, then add sugar little by little, and continue beating until fluffy.
4. Add eggs one by one, beat well after each addition. Continue beating until batter is creamy and smooth.
5. Then add sifted ingredients slowly, alternating with milk and vanilla, mixing until dry ingredients are incorporated.
6. Fill prepared muffin cups about three-quarters full and bake, rotating pans once, for 20–25 minutes, or until cupcakes spring back to the touch. Let cupcakes cool in tins about 5 minutes, then turn them out onto wire racks to cool completely. Decorate with your favorite frosting.

Ingredients

- 4 cups flour
- 5 teaspoons baking powder
- ¼ teaspoon salt
- 2 cups (4 sticks) butter
- 2 cups sugar
- 8 eggs
- 1½ cups milk
- 1 teaspoon vanilla

Difficulty
Easy

Baking Time
20–25 minutes

Portion
12 cupcakes

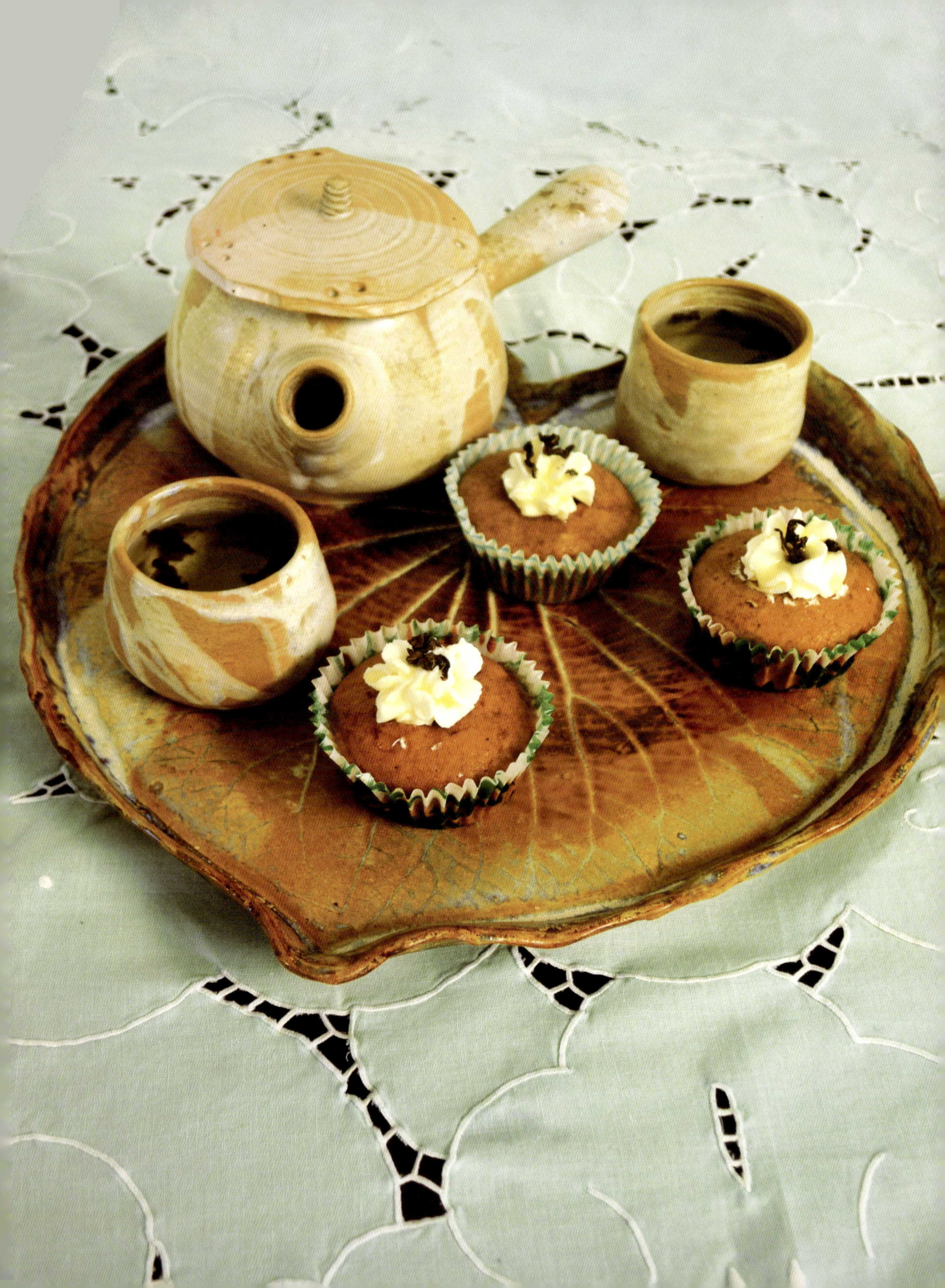

CHAI CUPCAKES

These moist cupcakes highlight the comforting flavors of a cup of tea—gently spiced chai in the cakes and delicate honey in the creamy topping.

Preparation

1. Preheat oven to 350°F. Line 12 muffin cups with paper or foil liners and set aside.
2. Make a strong cup of chai with the 3 tea bags and ⅔ cup of water and set aside to cool.
3. In a large bowl, combine sift the flour, brown sugar, baking soda, and salt.
4. In a medium bowl, stir together the melted butter, buttermilk, egg, and honey.
5. Add the wet ingredients (except for chai) to the dry ingredients, and mix on medium speed with an electric mixer or in the bowl of a stand mixer, 2 to 3 minutes until ingredients are blended. Add the cooled tea to the batter and mix just to combine.
6. Fill prepared muffin cups about two-thirds full and bake, rotating pans once, for 20 to 25 minutes, or until cupcakes spring back to the touch. Let cupcakes cool in tins about 5 minutes, then turn them out onto wire racks to cool completely.
7. Top with Honey Whipped Cream.

Ingredients

- 3 chai tea bags
- ⅔ cup hot water
- 1¼ cups flour
- ¼ cup brown sugar
- 1 teaspoon baking soda
- ¼ teaspoon salt
- ¼ cup butter, melted
- ¼ cup buttermilk
- 1 egg
- ¼ cup honey
- Honey Whipped Cream (recipe page 125)

Difficulty
Easy

Preparation Time
20–25 minutes

Portion
12 cupcakes

Cookies

- Chocolate Thumbprint Cookies with Strawberry Jelly
- Brownie Crinkles
- White Chocolate Cookies
- Mixed-Chip Cookies
- Oatmeal–Raisin Cookies
- Peanut Butter Cookies
- Sour Cream Cookies
- Spicy Dark Chocolate Cookies
- Ebony and Ivory Spirals and Marbles
- Delicate Almond Cookies
- Zesty Lemon Stars
- Linzer Hearts with Raspberry Jam
- Butter Cookies
- Black and White Sugar Cookies
- Gingerbread Cookies
- Sugar Cookie Cream Sandwiches

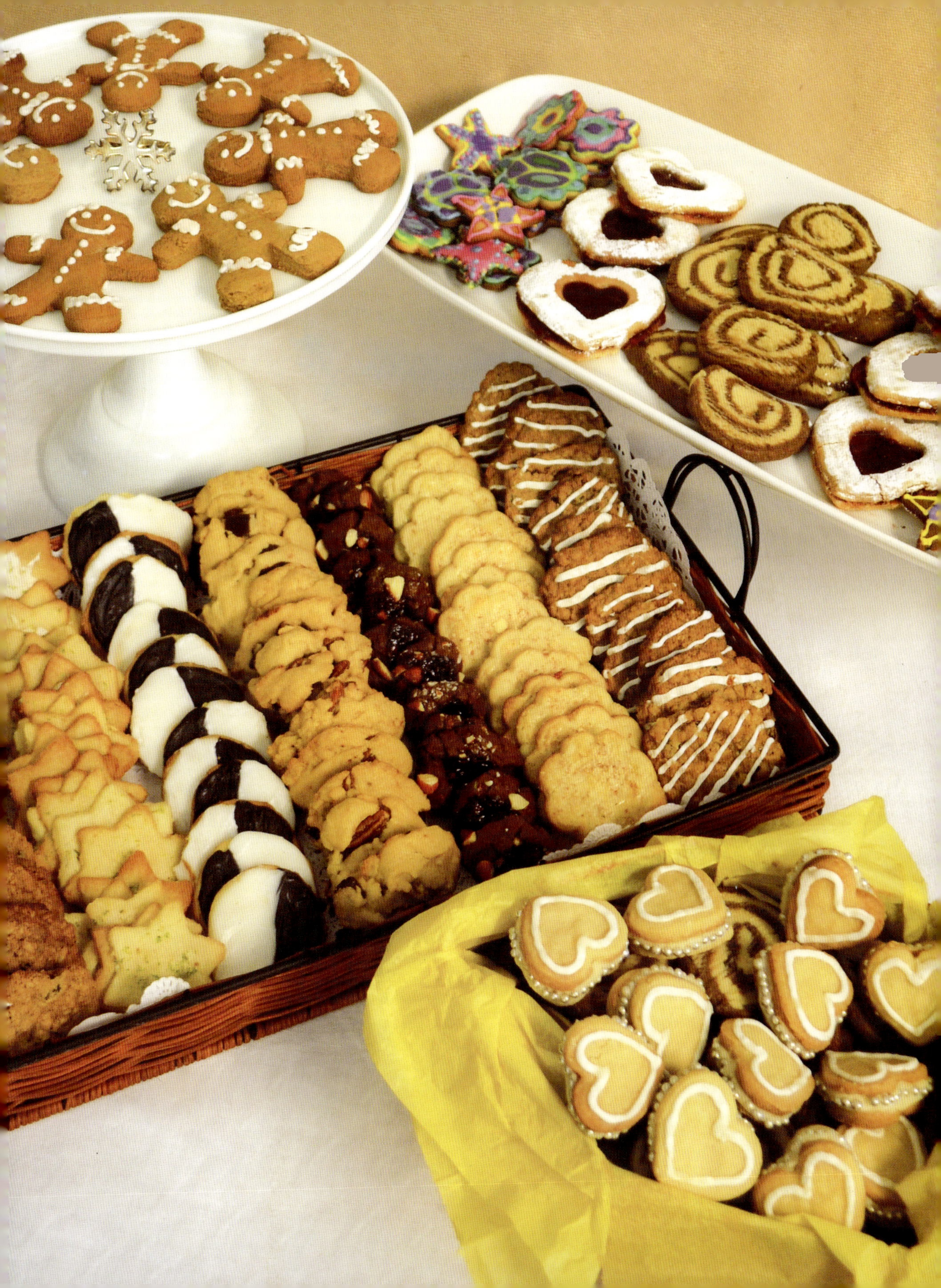

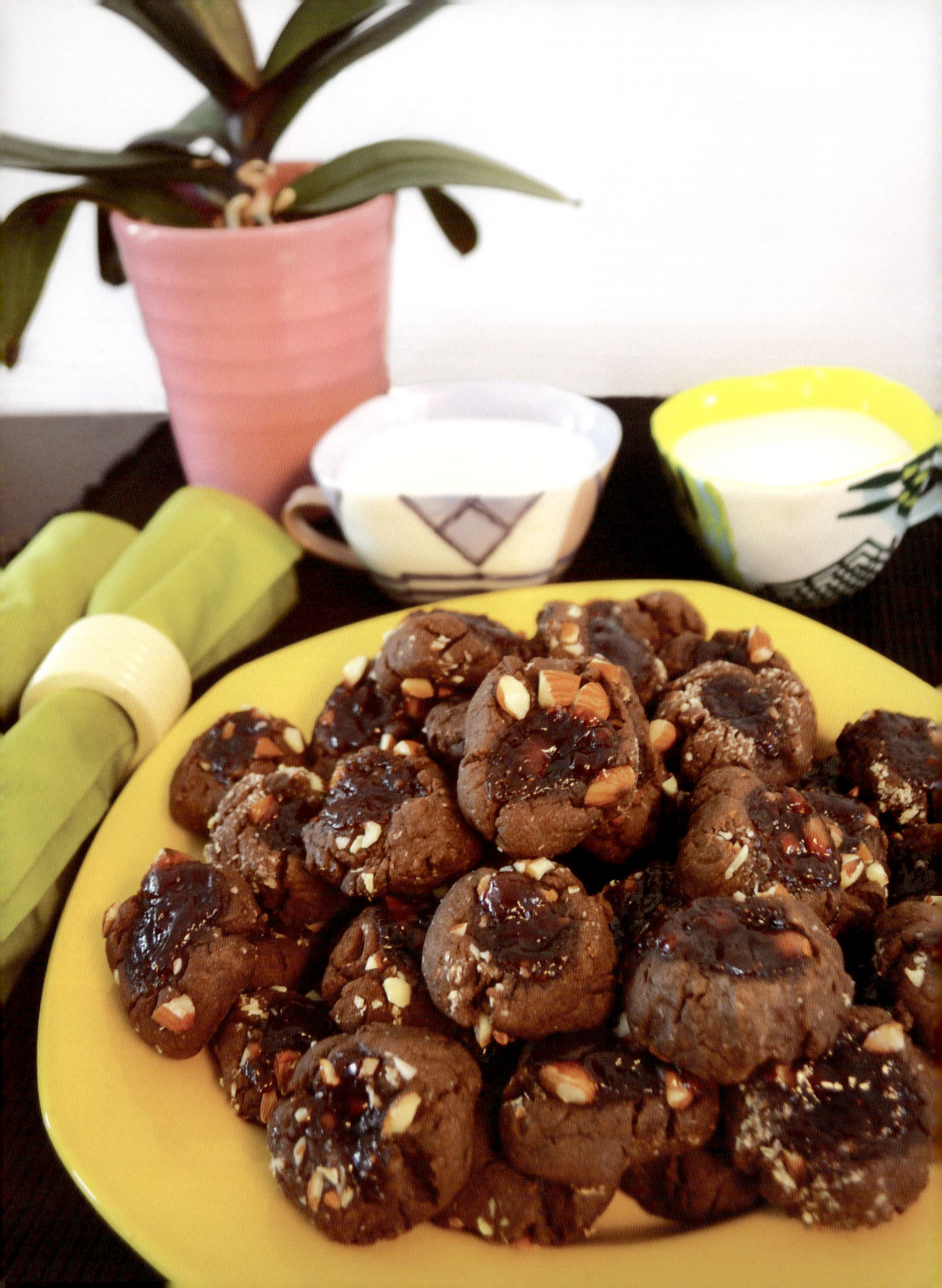

CHOCOLATE THUMBPRINT COOKIES WITH STRAWBERRY JELLY

Bite-sized morsels of joy! Thumbprint cookies are great fun for kids to make—and the chocolate flavor and strawberry filling are guaranteed child-pleasers.

Preparation

1. Sift together flour, baking soda, cocoa and salt. Set aside.
2. In a separate mixing bowl, using an electric mixer set on medium–high, cream together butter and sugar. Stir in egg and beat well. Add melted chocolate and vanilla and mix thoroughly.
3. Add sifted ingredients to mixture and blend well.
4. Using your hands, make one large ball of dough, wrap it in plastic wrap, and refrigerate for 1 hour.
5. When ready to bake, preheat oven to 350°F.
6. Spread chopped almonds over a sheet of wax paper. Form dough into 2-inch balls and roll each over chopped almonds. Place balls 1½ to 2 inches apart on ungreased baking sheet.
7. With your thumb, make a small indentation in each cookie and fill with ¼ teaspoon strawberry jam or jelly.
8. Bake for 15 minutes. Allow to cool on baking sheet for 5 minutes, then remove to wire rack to cool completely.

Ingredients

- 2⅔ cups all-purpose flour
- ¼ teaspoon baking soda
- ¼ teaspoon salt
- 1 cup (2 sticks) butter, softened
- ¾ cup sugar
- 1 egg
- 1 teaspoon vanilla extract
- ¼ cup cocoa
- 2 ounces unsweetened chocolate, melted
- ½ cups finely chopped almonds
- ½ cup strawberry jelly or jam

Difficulty
Easy

Baking Time
15 minutes

Portion
36 cookies

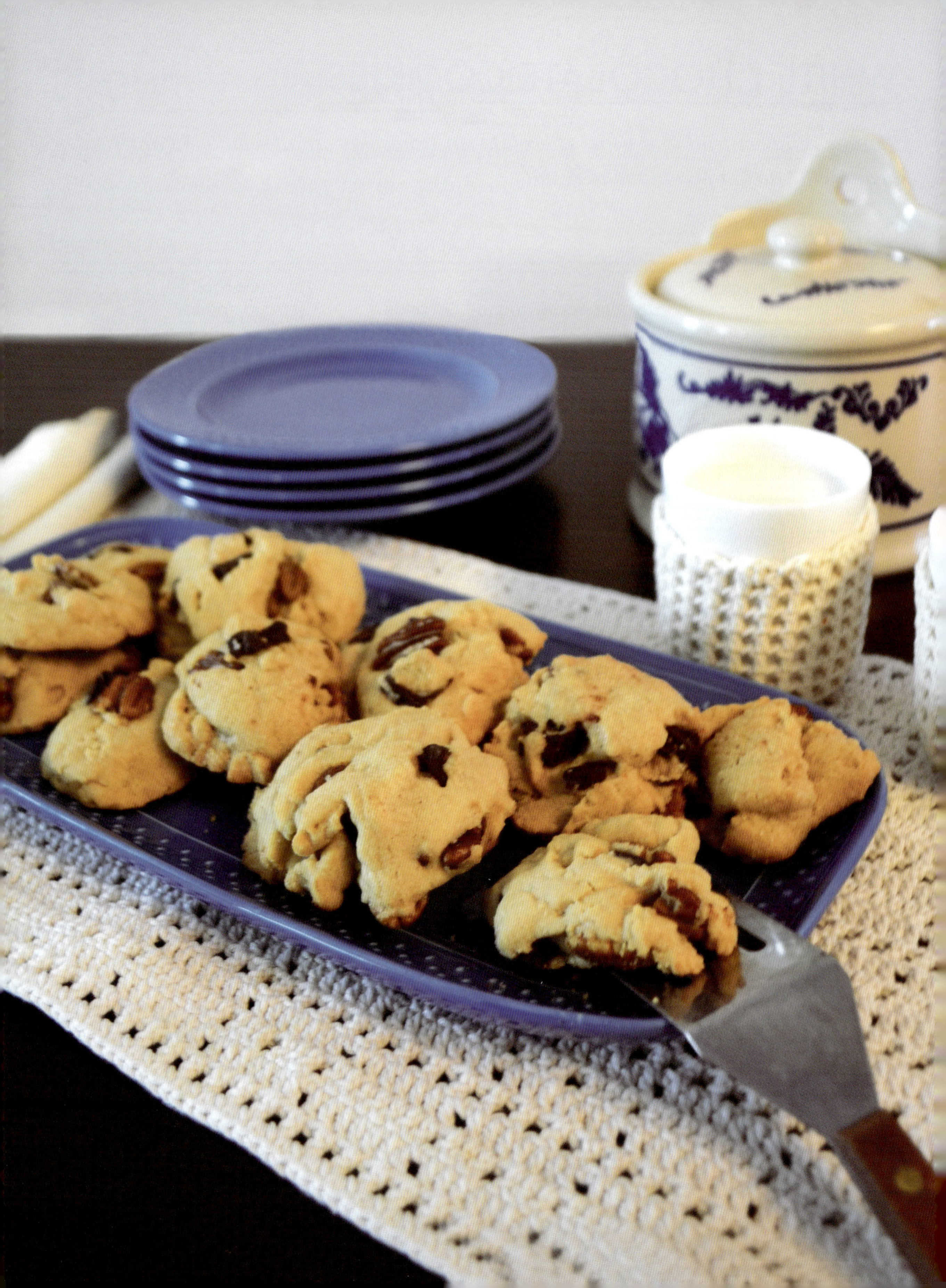

MIXED-CHIP COOKIES

I created this recipe when the pantry was running low—I had only small portions of white and dark chocolate chips left, and a few nuts. One inspired moment turned out an instant classic, now included for every party.

Preparation

1. Preheat oven to 350°F.
2. Sift together the flour, baking soda, and salt. Set aside.
3. In a separate mixing bowl, beat the butter, sugar, brown sugar, and eggs with an electric mixer set on low until creamy, about 5 to 8 minutes. Add vanilla and mix well.
4. Slowly beat sifted ingredients into the butter and sugar mixture.
5. Fold in walnuts, chocolate chips, and white chocolate chips.
6. Drop dough by rounded teaspoonfuls 2 inches apart on ungreased baking sheets.
7. Bake 15 minutes. Allow to cool on baking sheet for 2 minutes before removing to wire rack to cool completely.

Ingredients

- 4 cups flour
- 2 teaspoon baking soda
- ½ teaspoon salt
- 1½ cups butter (3 sticks), softened
- ½ cup sugar
- 1½ cups brown sugar
- 2 eggs
- 1 teaspoon vanilla extract
- 2 cups chopped walnuts
- 2 cups semisweet chocolate chips
- 1 cup white chocolate chips

Difficulty
Easy

Baking Time
15 minutes

Portion
36 cookies

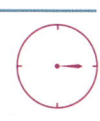

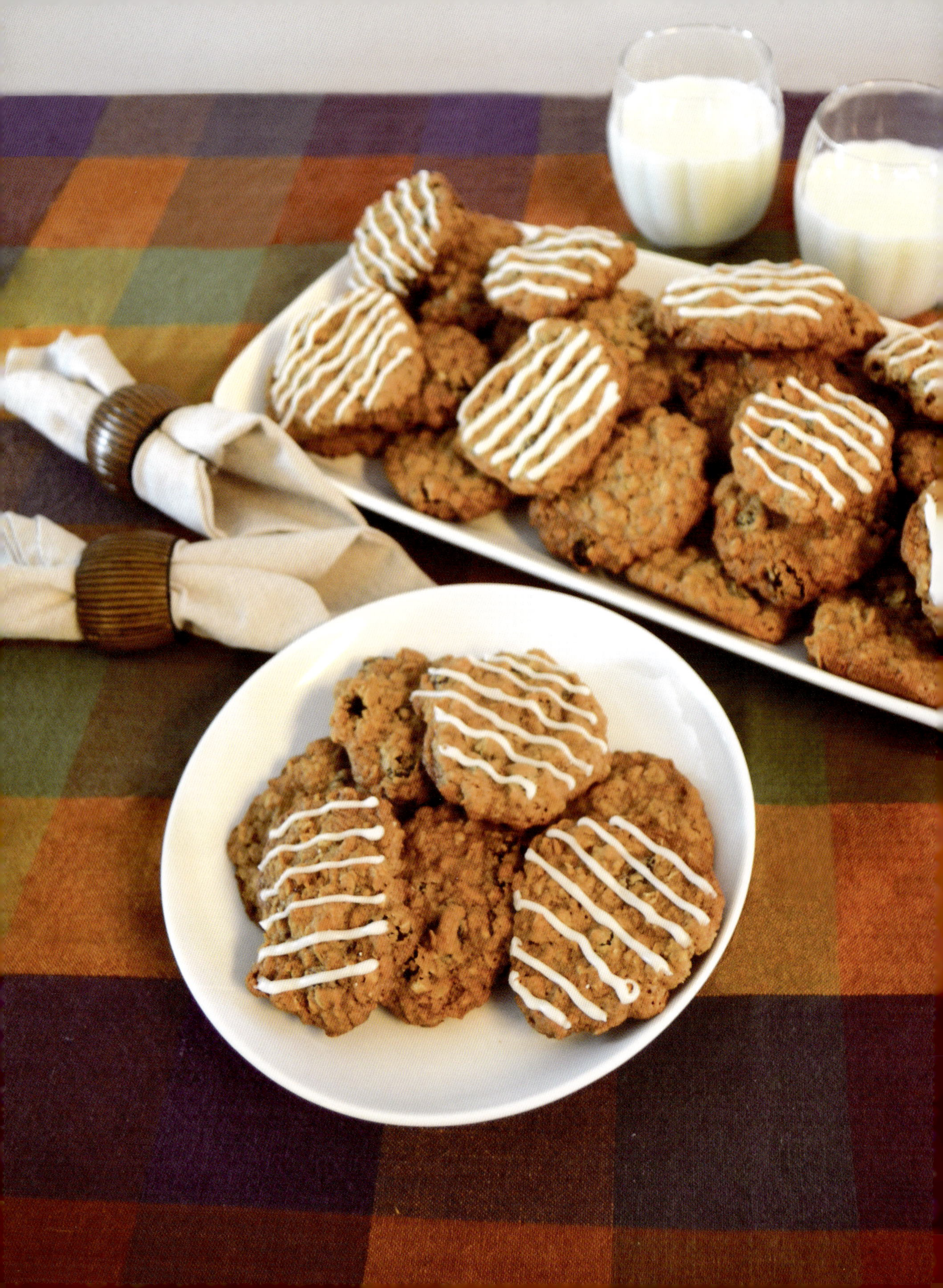

OATMEAL-RAISIN COOKIES

Soft, chewy, and simple to whip up, these are a go-to cookie for lunch boxes and afternoon snacks.

Preparation

1. Preheat oven to 350°F.
2. Sift together flour, baking soda, and salt. Set aside.
3. In a separate mixing bowl, beat butter with an electric mixer set to medium–high. Add brown sugar and granulated white sugar, continuing to beat until creamy. Beat in eggs and vanilla.
4. Add sifted dry ingredients to the wet ingredients and mix until well blended.
5. Stir in oats. Once oats are incorporated, gently fold in raisins.
6. Drop dough by teaspoonfuls 3 inches apart on ungreased cookie sheet. Bake 15 minutes or until golden brown. Cool on cookie sheets for 5 minutes, then remove to wire racks to cool completely.
7. Decorate with Confectioners' Sugar Icing.

Ingredients

- 1½ cups flour
- 1 teaspoon baking soda
- ½ teaspoon salt
- 1 cup butter (2 sticks), softened
- ¾ cup brown sugar
- ½ cup granulated white sugar
- 2 eggs
- 1 teaspoon vanilla extract
- 3 cups old-fashioned oats, uncooked
- 1 cup raisins
- Confectioners' Sugar Icing (recipe page 123)

Difficulty
Easy

Baking Time
15 minutes

Portion
24 cookies

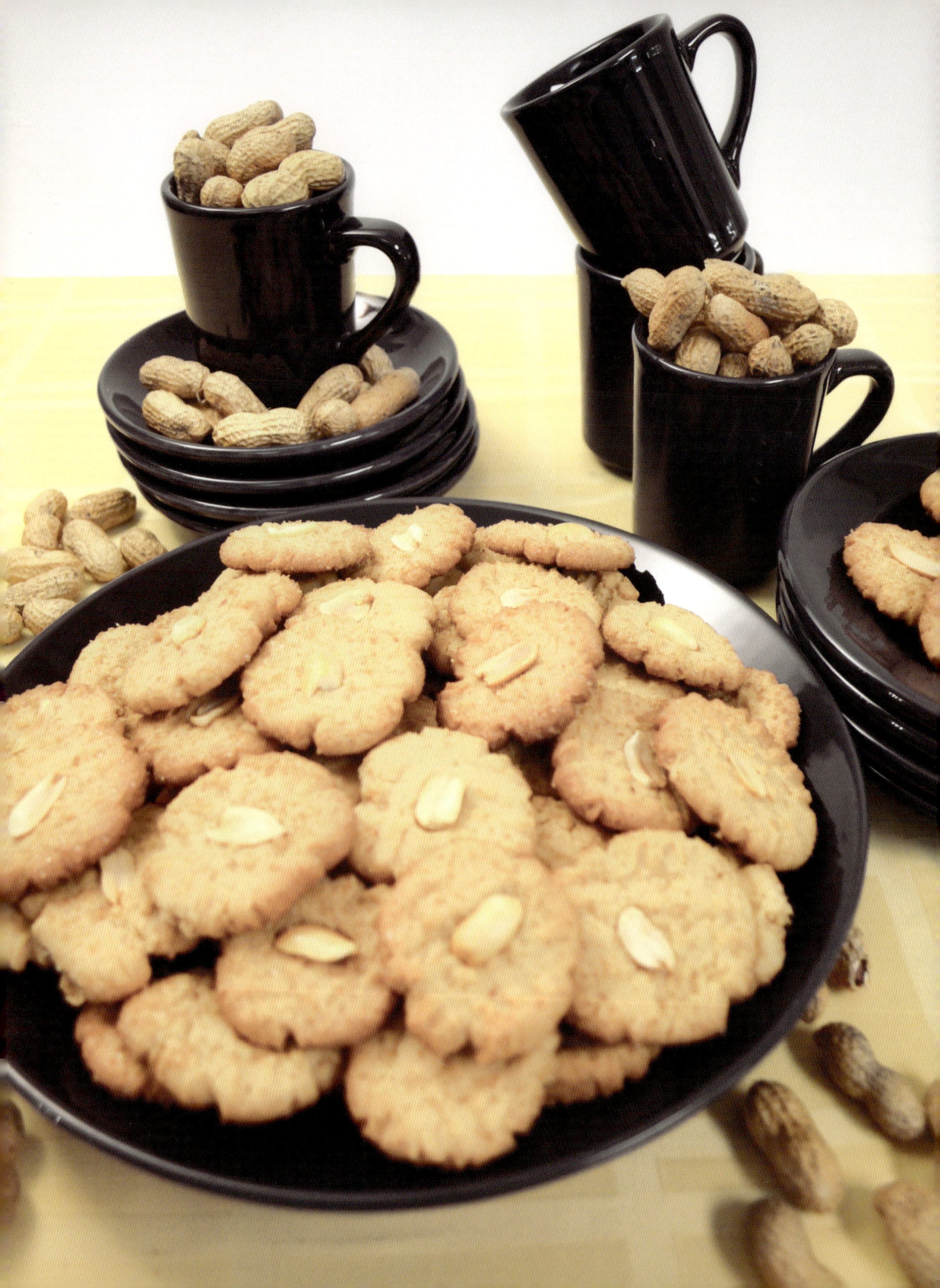

PEANUT BUTTER COOKIES

With their sweet-and-salty flavor and traditional crisscross pattern, these cookies are sure to be a hit with the peanut butter lovers in your life.

Preparation

1. Preheat oven to 375°F.
2. Using an electric mixer set on medium–high, cream together butter and peanut butter with white sugar, brown sugar, egg, and vanilla.
3. Add the flour, baking soda, and salt and mix until well blended.
4. Form teaspoon-sized balls of dough and roll them in white sugar. Add peanut halves to the middle of each cookie.
5. Place on ungreased baking sheet 2 inches apart. Press each ball with a fork to make a crosshatch design.
6.. Bake for 10 to 12 minutes or until golden brown. Allow to cool for 5 minutes then remove to wire rack to cool completely.

Ingredients

- ½ cup butter, softened
- ½ cup peanut butter
- ½ cup granulated white sugar, plus extra for coating
- ½ cup brown sugar
- 1 egg
- 1 teaspoon vanilla extract
- 1¼ cups flour
- ¾ teaspoon baking soda
- ¼ teaspoon salt
- optional: peanuts halves

Difficulty
Easy

Baking Time
10–12 minutes

Portion
24 cookies

SOUR CREAM COOKIES

These are flaky and light, a wonderful addition to your cookie repertoire. Its w simple ingredients make this recipe a great base for your creative experiments—try chopped apricots and almonds, miniature chocolate chips, or your favorite add-ins.

Ingredients

- 2¾ cups flour
- ½ teaspoon baking powder
- ½ teaspoon baking soda
- ½ teaspoon salt
- ½ cup butter (1 stick), softened
- 1½ cups sugar
- 2 eggs
- 1 cup sour cream
- 1 teaspoon vanilla extract

Preparation

1. Sift together the flour, baking powder, baking soda, and salt. Set aside.
2. In a separate mixing bowl, beat together butter, sugar, and eggs until creamy, about 5 to 6 minutes. Beat in sour cream and vanilla. Slowly mix dry ingredients into bowl until dough is well blended. Chill dough at least 1 hour.
3. When ready to bake, preheat oven to 400°F.
4. Drop rounded teaspoonfuls of dough 2 inches apart on ungreased baking sheet.
5. Bake 8 minutes. Allow to cool on baking sheet for 2 minutes before removing to wire rack to cool completely.

Difficulty
Easy

Baking Time
8 minutes

Portion
24 cookies

SPICY DARK CHOCOLATE COOKIES

Dark chocolate, candied ginger, and a blend of spices give this cookie a decidedly grown-up appeal—but you might be forced to share!

Preparation

1. Sift together the flour, ginger, pumpkin pie spice, and baking soda. Set aside.
2. In a separate mixing bowl, using an electric mixer set on medium-high, beat butter until fluffy. Add confectioners' sugar, continuing to beat.
3. Stir in melted chocolate and candied ginger.
4. Add sifted dry ingredients, mixing well.
5. Form dough into a ball, wrap in plastic wrap, and chill 2 hours.
6. When ready to bake, preheat oven to 350°F.
7. Form dough into teaspoon-sized balls and set 2 inches apart on ungreased baking sheets.
8. Bake 10 to 12 minutes.
9. Spread confectioners' sugar on a tray and roll still-warm cookies in the sugar (if cookies are too hot, allow them to cool until temperature allows for handling). Allow to cool on wire rack.

Ingredients

- 2 cups flour
- 1 teaspoon ground ginger
- 1 teaspoon pumpkin pie spice
- ¼ teaspoon ground cloves
- ½ teaspoon baking soda
- 1 cup (2 sticks) butter, softened
- 1 cup confectioners' sugar, sifted, plus additional for rolling
- 4 ounces unsweetened chocolate, melted
- 1 teaspoon chopped candied ginger

Difficulty
Easy

Baking Time
12 minutes

Portion
24 cookies

EBONY AND IVORY SPIRALS AND MARBLES

It takes a little effort to get the spiral pattern down, but these deliciously simple cookies definitely bring the wow factor.

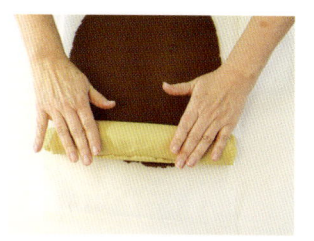

Preparation

1. Sift together flour and salt. Set aside.
2. In a separate mixing bowl, with an electric mixer set on medium, beat butter with confectioners' sugar and egg until creamy.
3. Add sifted flour and salt to the butter and sugar and beat well.
4. Divide dough into two equal parts. To one half add cocoa and buttermilk and blend well.
5. On a sheet of waxed paper, roll chocolate dough into a 10-by-6½-inch rectangle. Roll white dough into a 10-by-6 ½-inch rectangle. Place white dough on top of chocolate dough.
6. Using wax paper to help, roll the two layers of dough together into a log. Press seam well and chill for 2 hours or until firm.
7. When ready to bake, preheat oven to 350°F. Cut roll into ¼-inch slices and place 1½ inch apart on ungreased baking sheet. Bake for 8 to 10 minutes. Let cool on baking sheet for 5 minutes before removing to a wire rack to cool.
8. Roll the leftover dough into ballls and flatten, bake as above.

Ingredients

- 2⅔ cups flour
- 1 teaspoon salt
- 1 cup butter
- 1½ cups confectioners' sugar
- 1 egg
- ¼ cup cocoa
- 1 tablespoon buttermilk

Difficulty
Intermediate

Baking Time
8–10 minutes

Portion
24 cookies

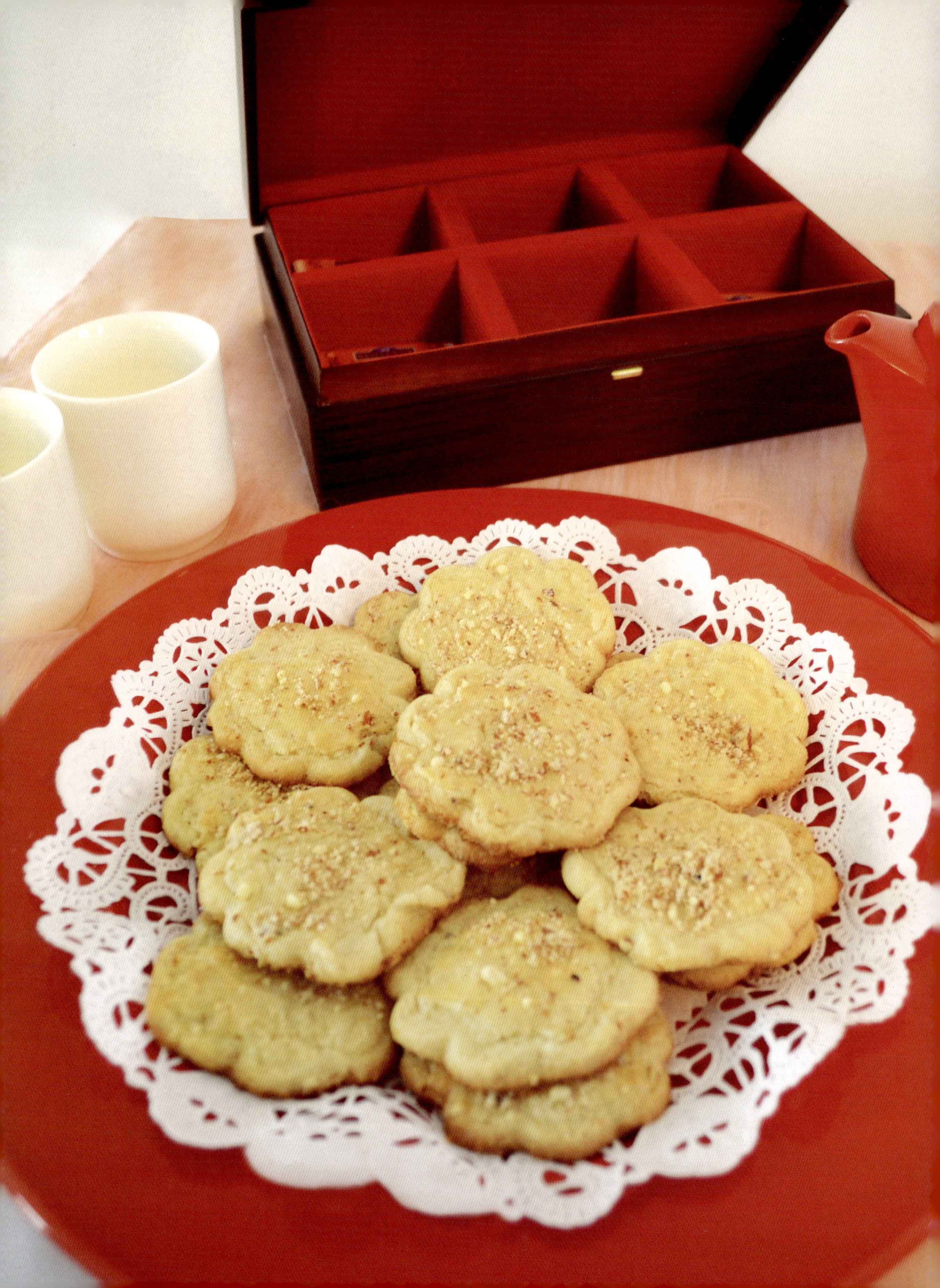

DELICATE ALMOND COOKIES

These are a family favorite at Christmastime. Full of flavor and with a sweet aroma, they grace our holiday cookie plate every year.

Preparation

1. Grind the almonds very fine.
2. In a separate mixing bowl, using an electric mixer set on medium–high beat butter until fluffy. Stir in confectioners' sugar and continue beating until creamy.
3. Mix three quarters of the ground almonds into the flour and stir dry ingredients into the butter and sugar mixture.
4. Form dough into a ball and chill 2 to 3 hours.
5. When ready to bake, preheat oven to 350°F.
6. On a floured surface, roll the dough out to ¼-inch thickness and cut with cookie cutter, using round, square, flower, or any desired shape.
7. Beat egg whites with a fork. Brush each cookie with egg white and sprinkle with remaining ground almonds. Place on an ungreased baking sheet 1 inch apart. Bake for 8 to 10 minutes or until golden. Cool on baking sheet for 5 minutes before removing to wire rack to cool completely.

Ingredients

- ½ cup almonds
- 1½ cups (3 sticks) butter, softened
- 2 cups confectioners' sugar, sifted
- 2 cups flour
- 2 egg whites

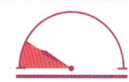

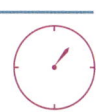

Difficulty
Easy

Baking Time
8–10 minutes

Portion
36 cookies

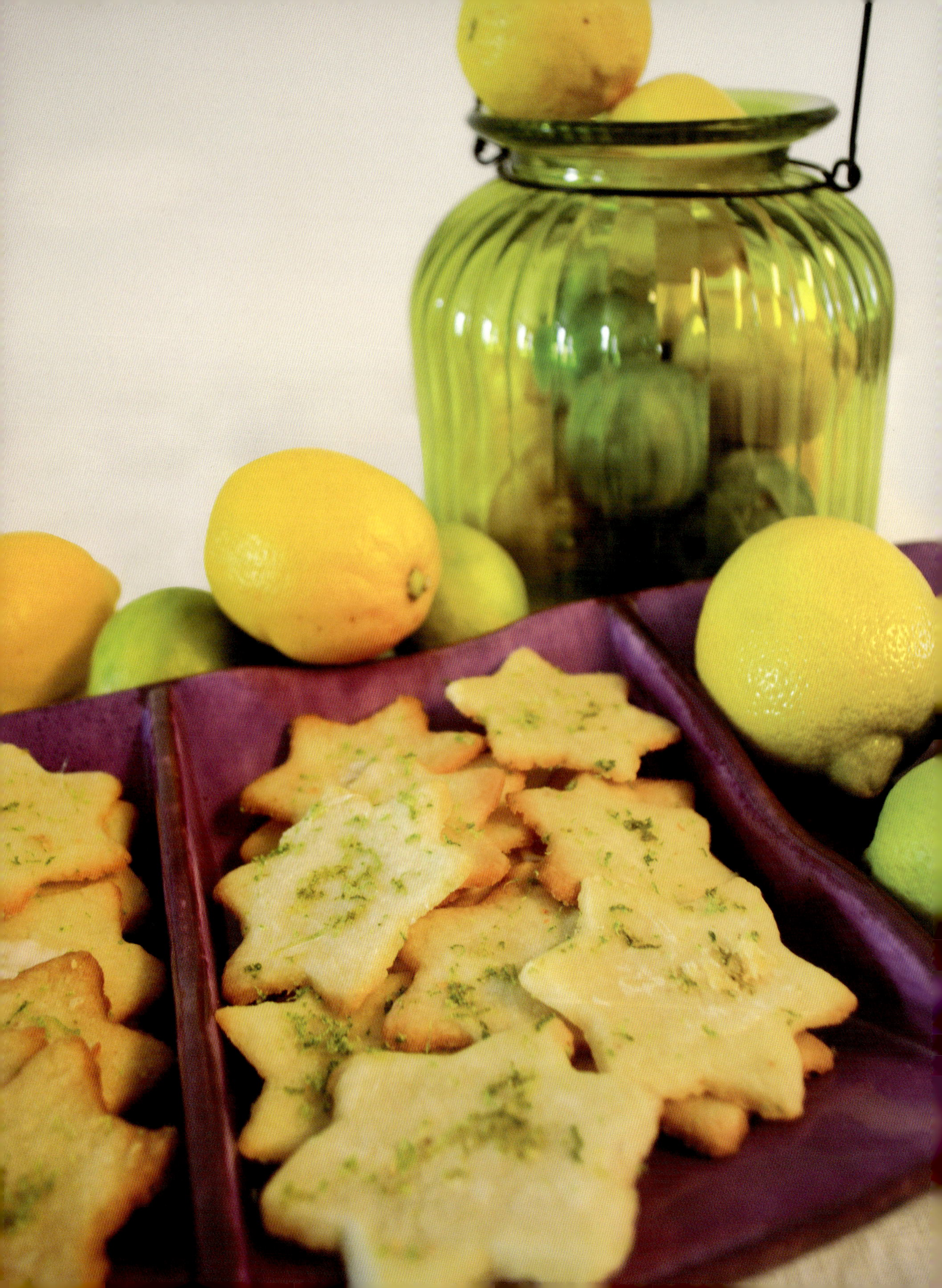

ZESTY LEMON STARS

Exquisite lemon flavor and a pretty shape make these luscious cookies the star of your spring baking!

Preparation

1. Preheat oven to 350°F.
2. Sift together flour, salt, and baking powder and set aside.
3. In a separate mixing bowl, with an electric mixer set on medium–high, cream the butter and sugar. Add the 3 eggs and half of the lemon zest, and stir with a fork to blend.
4. Add the sifted dry ingredients to the wet ingredients and work the dough with your hands until well combined.
5. On a floured surface, roll the dough out to ¼ inch. Cut dough into star shapes with a cookie cutter and place on an ungreased baking sheet. Whisk the egg white with a fork and brush each cookie with a light coat. Sprinkle each cookie with lemon zest.
6. Bake for 8 minutes or until golden. Allow to cool for 5 minutes on baking sheet, then remove to wire rack to cool completely.

Ingredients

- 3 cups flour
- 1 teaspoon baking powder
- ¼ teaspoon salt
- 1 cup butter
- ¼ cup sugar
- 3 eggs
- 1 egg white
- Zest of 2 lemons

Difficulty
Easy

Baking Time
8 minutes

Portion
24 cookies

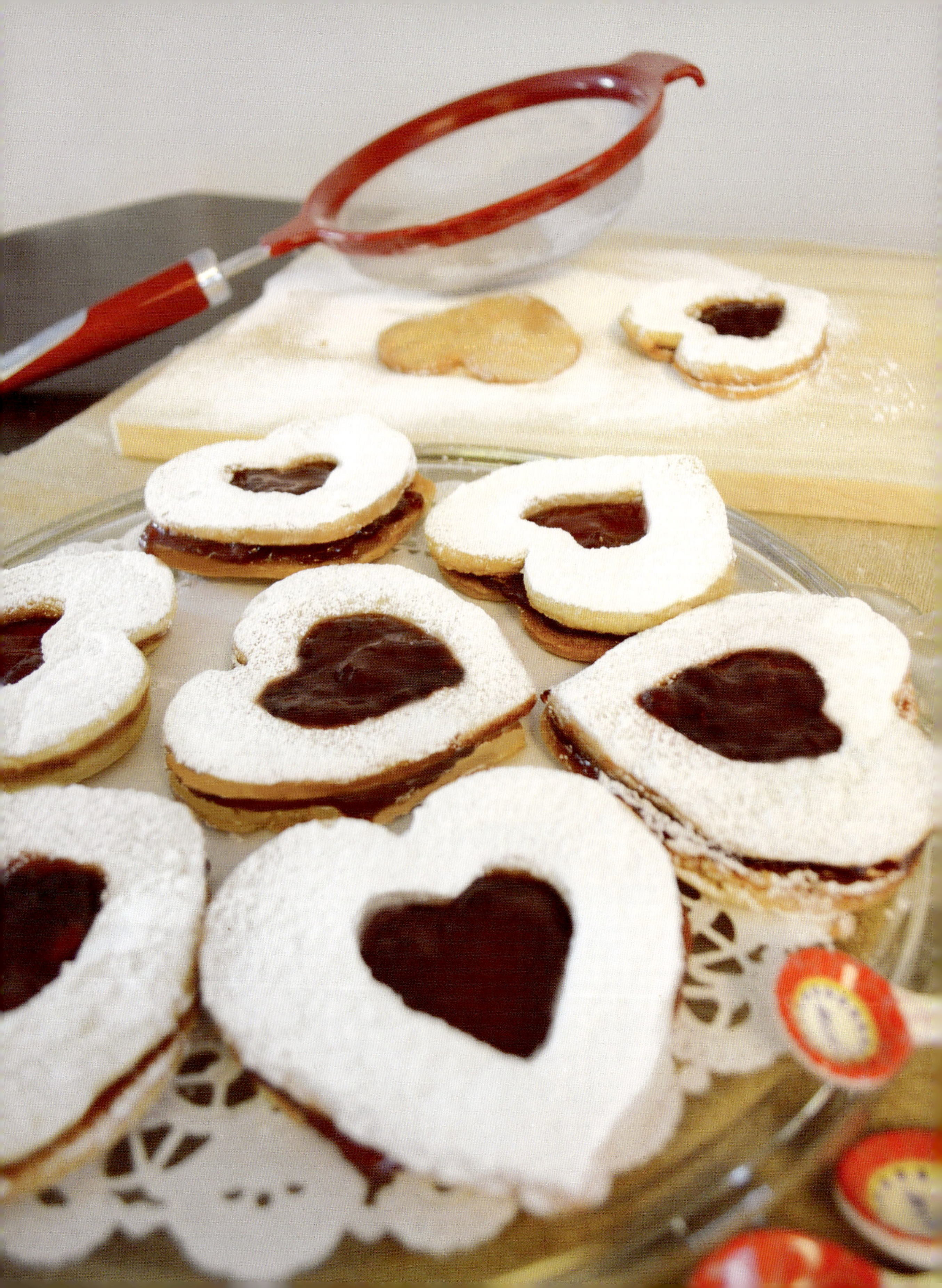

LINZER HEARTS WITH RASPBERRY JAM

These romantic cookies take a little effort, but they're worth it! Try other jams and jellies as filling—any thick jam will work beautifully.

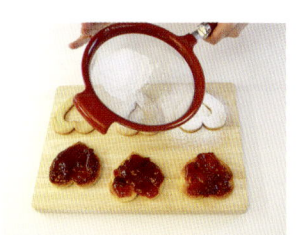

Preparation

1. Cream together the butter and sugar, using an electric mixer set on medium–high. Add sifted flour slowly to the butter and sugar, mixing well with hands to form a smooth dough.
2. Divide the dough into two parts and wrap in plactic wrap. Chill in the refrigerator for at least 1 hour.
3. When ready to bake, preheat oven to 350°F and linebaking sheet with parchment paper.
4. Using a rolling pin, roll out one ball of dough to ¼-inch thickness. Use large heart-shaped cookie cutter to cut out cookies. These will be the bottoms. Place them 1 inch apart on baking sheet. Roll out the other ball of dough; use same cookie cutter to make equal number of cookies. For this batch, use a smaller heart-shaped cookie cutter to cut out the center of each cookie. These will be the tops—The cookies with the heart-shaped holes will be the top of the "cookie sandwich."
5. Bake for 12 minutes or until golden. Cool for 5 minutes on baking sheet then remove to wire rack to cool completely.
6. Once cookies have cooled, spread bottoms with raspberry jam. Sift confectioners' sugar over tops, then place tops on the jam-covered bottoms to form a sandwich cookie.

Ingredients

- 1 cup (2 sticks) butter, softened
- 1 cup sugar
- 2½ cups flour, sifted
- ½ cup confectioners' sugar
- Raspberry jam*

*Substitute your favorite jam or jelly—strawberry and apricot work well—for the raspberry in the recipe.

Difficulty
Intermediate

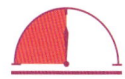

Baking Time
12 minutes

Portion
12 cookies

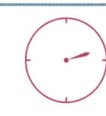

85

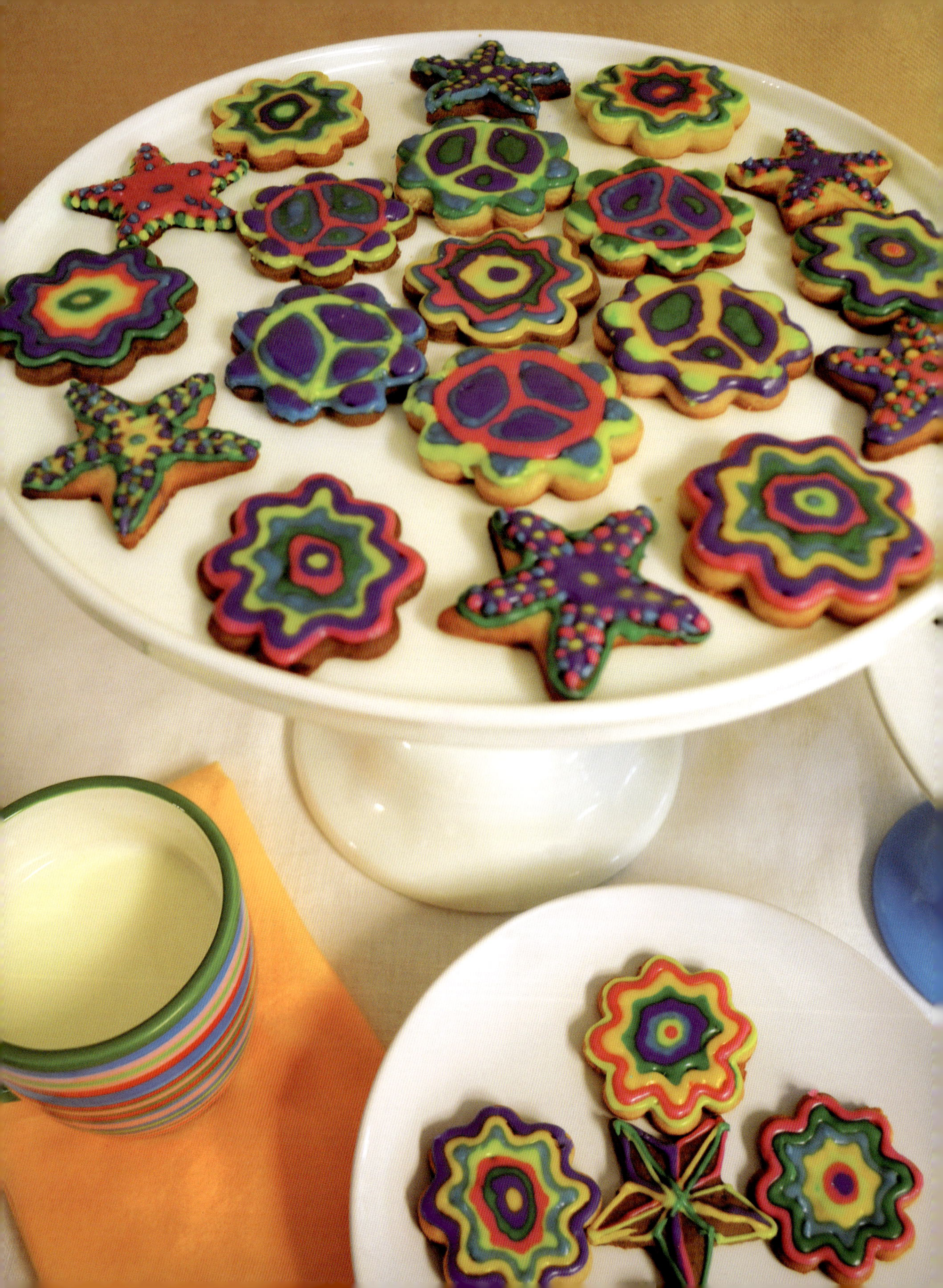

BUTTER COOKIES

These rich cookies are rolled out and shaped with cookie cutters, so they're easy to make. Have fun decorating them with colored icing to make them festive!

Preparation

1. Preheat the oven to 350°F.
2. Mix together the butter and sugar, then add egg yolks.
3. Mix in the flour and vanilla or almond extract, preferably working the dough with your hands.
4. Form dough into teaspoon-sized balls. Place them 1 inch apart on an ungreased baking sheet.
5. Bake 10 to 12 minutes or until golden. Cool on baking sheet for 5 minutes, then remove to a wire rack to cool completely.
6. Decorate with *Confectioners' Sugar Icing*.

Ingredients

- 1 cup butter (2 sticks), softened
- ⅔ cup sugar
- 3 egg yolks
- 2½ cups flour
- 1 teaspoon vanilla extract or almond extract
- *Confectioners' Sugar Icing (recipe page 123)*

Difficulty
Easy

Baking Time
10–12 minutes

Portion
36 cookies

BLACK AND WHITE SUGAR COOKIES

Perfect plain or dressed up with black and white icing, this recipe uses ingredients you're likely to have on hand. So when the baking mood strikes, turn to this tasty standby!

Preparation

1. Preheat oven to 350°F. Line baking sheets with parchment paper, if desired.
2. Cream butter and sugar together using an electric mixer set on low speed for 5 minutes. Beat in egg and vanilla.
3. Slowly mix sifted flour into the bowl with butter and sugar, scraping down sides as necessary.
4. Form dough into small balls, each about the size of rounded teaspoonful, and place them 2 inches apart on a baking sheet.
5. Flatten the balls gently with the palm of your hand crosswise or with the back of a large spoon.
6. Bake 10 to 12 minutes, or until golden. Let cool 2 minutes on baking sheet, then remove to a wire rack to cool completely.
7. Decorate with a knife or brush, using Confectioners' Sugar (white and chocolate) or Ganache.

Ingredients

- 1 cup butter (2 sticks), softened
- 1 cup sugar
- 1 egg
- 1 teaspoon vanilla extract
- 2¼ cups flour, sifted
- Confectioners' Sugar Icing (recipe page 123)
- Ganache (recipe page 133)

Difficulty
Intermediate

Baking Time
10-12 minutes

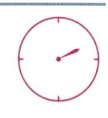

Portion
36 cookies

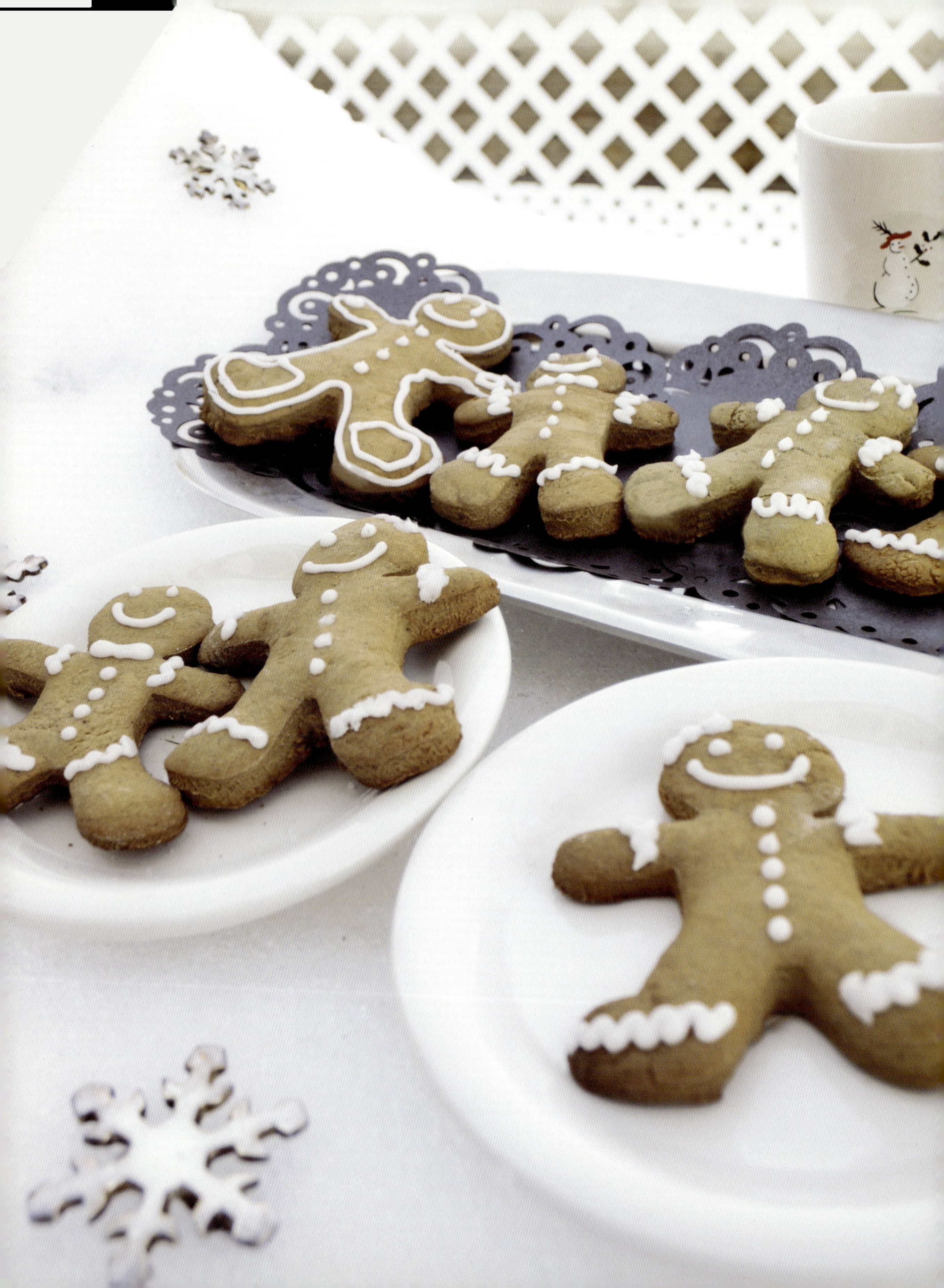

GINGERBREAD COOKIES

This is my mother's traditional recipe—my family has had a lot of fun decorating these cookies over many Christmases! They are delicious served with hot cocoa on a snowy day.

Preparation

1. Sift together the flour, salt, cinnamon, ginger, allspice, and cloves. Set aside.
2. In a separate mixing bowl, beat butter using an electric mixer set on medium–high, then add brown sugar and continue mixing. Add molasses and cold water, and mix.
3. Stir sifted ingredients into the butter and brown sugar mixture until dough forms.
4. Add the baking soda dissolved in water and the candied ginger and beat well.
5. Chill dough, tightly covered, in refrigerator overnight.
6. When ready to bake, preheat oven to 350°F. Grease baking sheet and set aside.
7. On a floured surface, roll dough out to about ½-inch thickness. Use a gingerbread man or woman cookie cutter to form cookies.
8. Bake 18 minutes or until cookies spring back when touched.
9. Decorate with Confectioners' Sugar Icing.

Ingredients

- 7 cups flour
- 1 teaspoon salt
- 1 teaspoon cinnamon
- 1 teaspoon ground ginger
- 1 teaspoon ground allspice
- 1 teaspoon ground cloves
- ⅓ cup butter, softened
- 1 cup brown sugar
- 1¼ cups dark molasses
- ½ cup cold water
- 2 teaspoons baking soda dissolved in 3 tablespoons cold water
- ¼ cup chopped candied ginger
- *Confectioners' Sugar Icing (recipe page 123)*

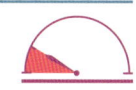

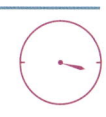

Difficulty
Easy

Baking Time
18 minutes

Portion
12 large cookies

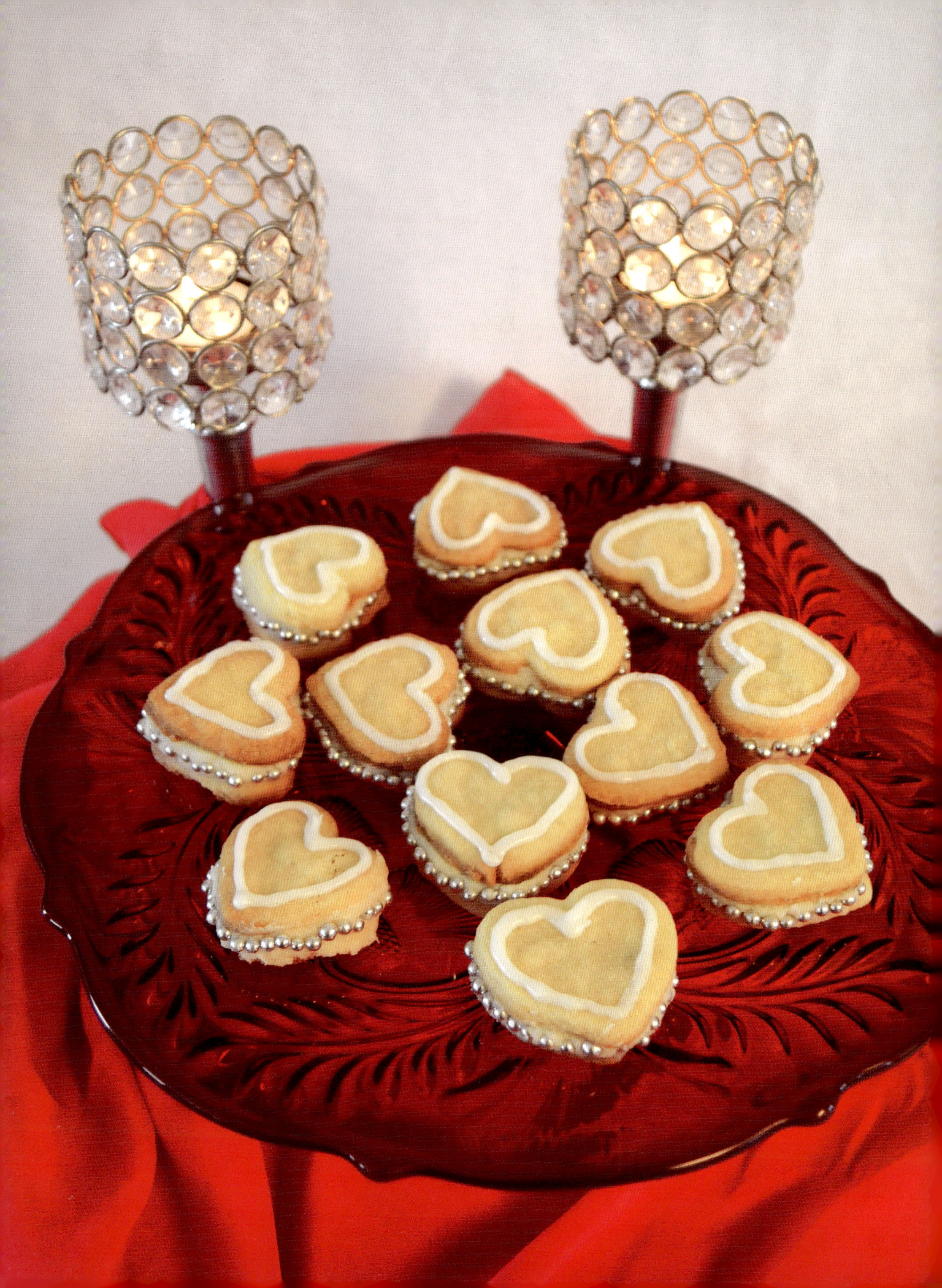

SUGAR COOKIE CREAM SANDWICHES

Crispy outside, soft and creamy inside, these little gems will beat out your favorite store-bought sandwich cookies every time.

Preparation

1. Preheat oven to 350°F.
2. In a mixing bowl, using an electric mixer set on medium-high, beat together butter and sugar until creamy. Add egg and vanilla and beat well.
3. Stir in flour until ingredients are well combined, beating slowly or folding with spatula.
4. Roll out on floured surface to ¼ inch thick and cut into desired shapes with cookie cutters. Alternatively, form dough into small balls and place them 2 inches apart on an ungreased baking sheet. Flatten balls gently with a fork, pressing crosswise to make a grid pattern.
5. Bake 10 to 12 minutes or until golden. Cool 5 minutes on baking sheet before removing to wire rack.
6. Once cookies are completely cool, spread half the cookies with 1 teaspoon *Easy Buttercream Frosting* and top with the remaining cookies to form a cream-filled sandwich. Decorate, if desired, with piped frosting for tops and sprinkles, draggees, or other embellishments for the cream sides.

Ingredients

- ½ cup (1 stick) butter, softened
- 2 teaspoons of lemon juice
- 1 cup sugar
- 1 egg
- 1 teaspoon vanilla
- 2¼ cups flour, sifted
- *Easy Buttercream Frosting (recipe page 121)*

Difficulty
Easy to intermediate

Preparation Time
10-12 minutes

Portion
36 cookies

Biscotti & Bars

- Cinnamon and Coffee Bars
- Brownie Bars with Fudge Icing
- Coconut-Toffee Bars
- Classic Chocolate Brownies
- Cranberry-Orange Shortbreads
- Chocolate-Dipped Nut Biscotti
- Pistachio Biscotti

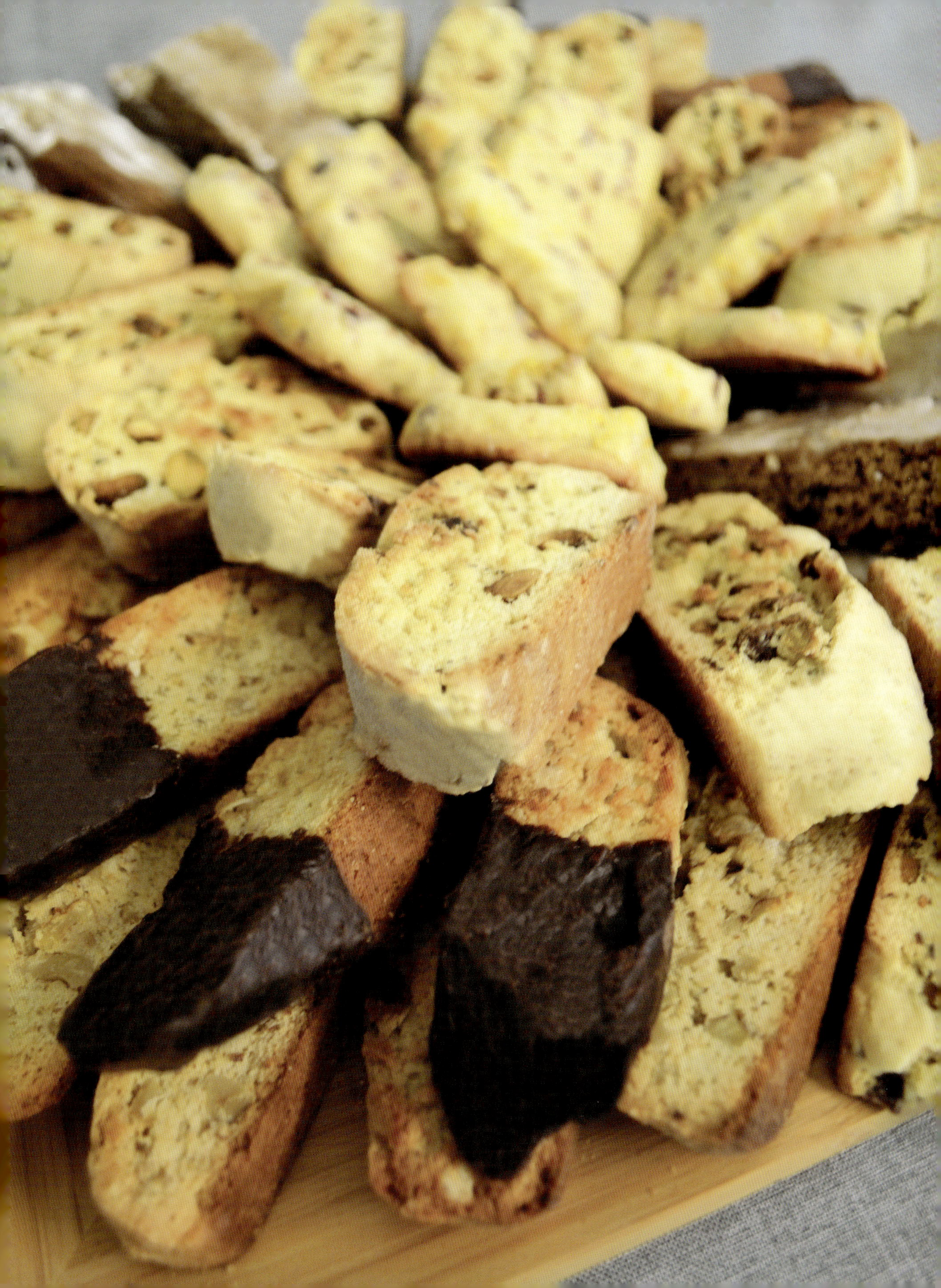

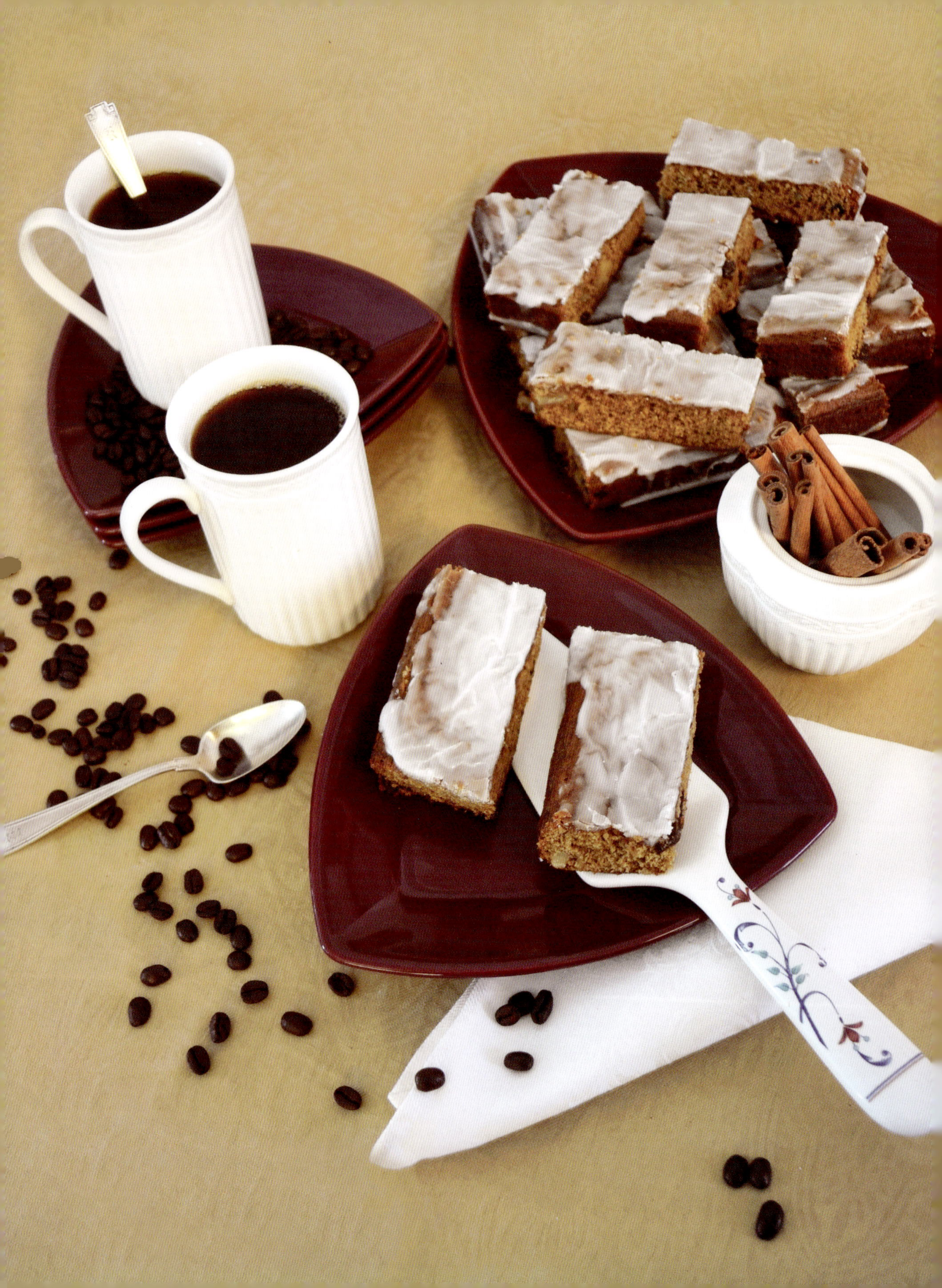

CINNAMON AND COFFEE BARS

These delicious bars are infused with the homey flavors of coffee and cinnamon—they are especially welcome at holiday time, but are delightful all year round.

Preparation

1. Preheat oven to 350°F. Grease a 13-by-9-inch glass baking dish and set aside.
2. Brew black coffee with cinnamon sticks (place cinnamon sticks in coffee filter). Set aside.
3. Using an electric mixer set on medium-high, beat butter until light and fluffy.
4. Add brown sugar then egg to the butter mixture and beat well.
5. When mixture is creamy, stop the beater and stir in the hot coffee.
6. In a separate bowl, sift together the flour, baking powder, and ground cinnamon.
7. Add the sifted dry ingredients to the butter mixture and mix well. Fold in raisins and walnuts.
8. Spread batter in prepared pan and bake for 20 minutes, or until a toothpick inserted in the middle comes out clean.
9. While the bars are still warm, drizzle the top with the Confectioners' Cugar Icing. Cut into bars.

Ingredients

- ½ cup strong black coffee
- 2 cinnamon sticks
- ¼ cup butter
- 1 cup brown sugar
- 1 egg
- 1½ cups flour
- 1 teaspoon baking powder
- ¼ teaspoon ground cinnamon
- ½ cup raisins
- ½ cup chopped walnuts
- *Confectioners' Sugar Icing (recipe page 123)*

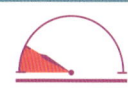

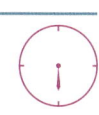

Difficulty
Easy

Baking Time
20 minutes

Portion
16 servings

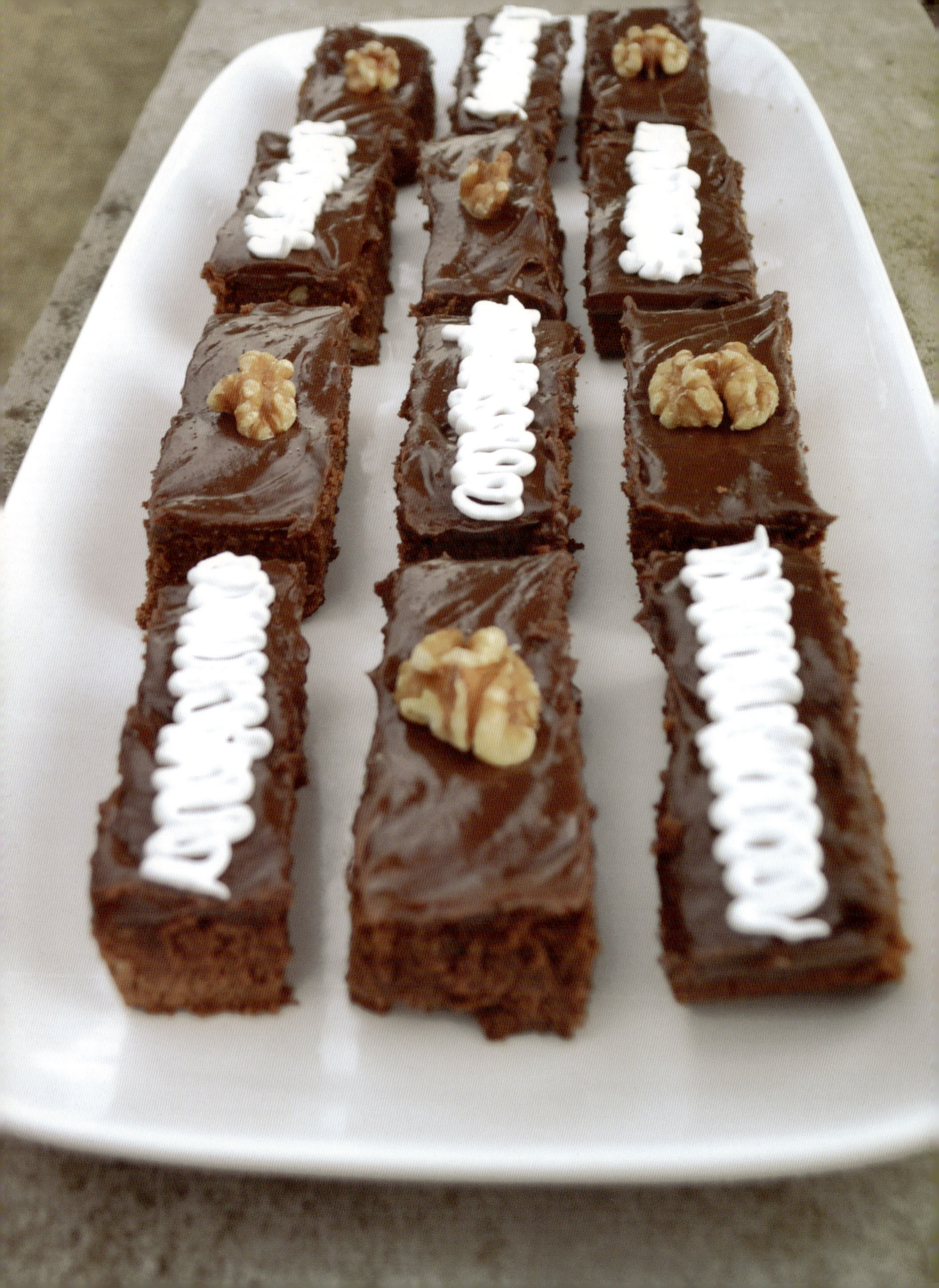

BROWNIE BARS WITH FUDGE ICING

These decadent brownies go completely over the top when frosted with Fudge Icing. Serve them with vanilla or pistachio ice cream for a truly special treat!

Preparation

1. Preheat oven to 350°F. Grease an 8-by-8 pan and set aside.
2. In a large mixing bowl, sift together the flour, baking powder, and salt. Set aside.
3. Melt butter in a saucepan over medium-low heat, then add cocoa powder and stir to make a chocolate sauce. Be careful not to burn the chocolate.
4. In a separate mixing bowl, beat eggs with an electric mixer set on low until soft peaks form. Add sugar and continue beating until well mixed.
5. Stir in melted butter and chocolate and mix well.
6. Add sifted ingredients and mix until just combined.
7. Spread batter in prepared pan and bake 30 minutes, or until a toothpick inserted in the middle comes out clean. Allow to cool in pan.
8. Frost with Fudge Icing and cut into squares. Decorate as desired.

Ingredients

- ¾ cup flour
- 1 teaspoon baking powder
- ½ teaspoon salt
- ⅓ cup butter
- ½ cup cocoa powder
- 2 eggs
- 1 cup sugar
- ½ cup chopped walnuts
- *Fudge Icing (recipe page 131)*

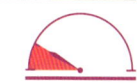

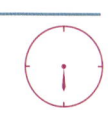

Difficulty
Easy

Baking Time
30 minutes

Portion
16 servings

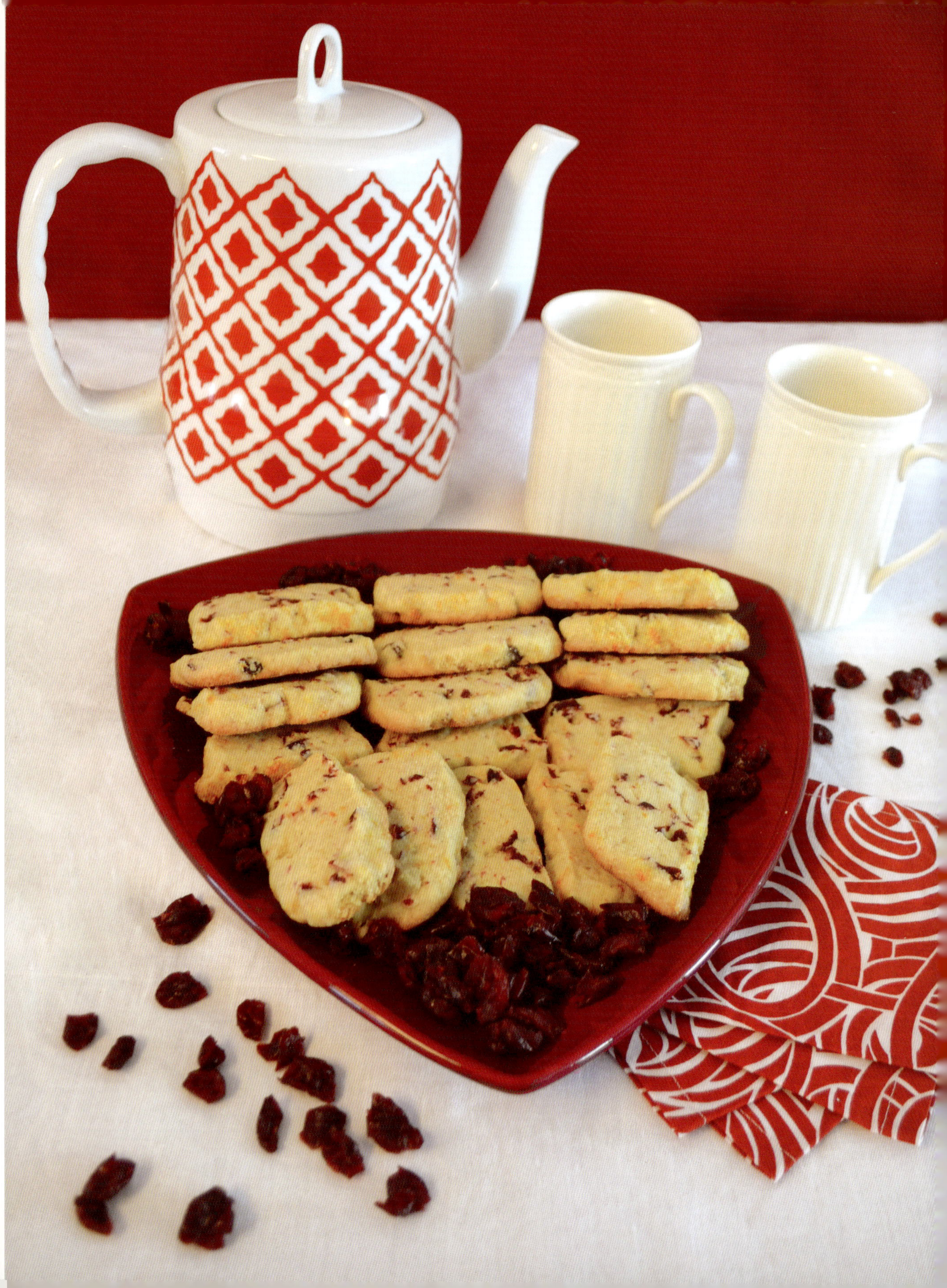

CRANBERRY-ORANGE SHORTBREADS

These festive cookies capture the homey flavors of winter, with piquant orange zest and cranberries paired with pumpkin pie spice.

Preparation

1. Sift together flour, baking soda, salt, and pumpkin pie spice. Set aside.
2. In a separate mixing bowl, beat butter and sugar together with an electric mixer set on medium–high until creamy, occasionally scraping bowl with spatula. Add egg and vanilla; beat until well mixed.
3. Reduce speed to low and gradually beat in sifted dry ingredients, just until blended. Fold in cranberries and orange peel.
4. Divide dough in half. On lightly floured surface, with hands, shape each half into a 10-inch-long log. Using hands or two clean rulers on the log sides, press each log into a 10-inch-long squared-off shape. Wrap each log in plastic wrap and chill until firm enough to slice, 2 hours in freezer or overnight in refrigerator.
5. When ready to bake, preheat oven to 350°F.
6. Spread 3 tablespoons of sanding sugar and 1 teaspoon of grated orange peel on a sheet of waxed paper. Unwrap 1 log and press sides in sugar to coat. Cut log into ¼-inch-thick slices. Place slices, 1 inch apart, on ungreased cookie sheet. Repeat with second log.
7. Bake 14 to 16 minutes or until golden. Transfer shortbread to wire rack to cool.

Ingredients

- 2¾ cups flour
- ¼ teaspoon baking soda
- ¼ teaspoon salt
- 1 teaspoon pumpkin pie spice
- 1 cup (2 sticks) butter, softened
- ¾ cup sugar
- 1 large egg
- 1 teaspoon vanilla extract
- ½ cup dried cranberries, finely chopped
- 2 teaspoons grated fresh orange peel for batter
- 6 tablespoons sanding sugar or other coarse sugar
- 1 teaspoons grated fresh orange peel for topping

Difficulty
Easy to Intermediate

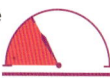

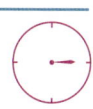

Baking Time
14–16 minutes

Portion
20–24 servings

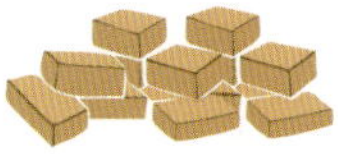

CHOCOLATE-DIPPED NUT BISCOTTI

Irresistible with a cup of coffee, these crisp biscotti offer just the right amount of sweetness, thanks to their dipped-chocolate ends.

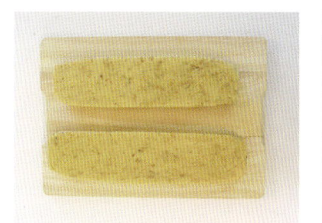

Preparation

1. Spread nuts evenly over baking sheet and bake for 8 minutes at 350°F, until lightly toasted. Set aside.
2. Sift together the flour and baking powder and set aside.
3. In a separate mixing bowl, using an electric mixer set on medium–high, beat butter until fluffy. Add sugar and eggs, one a time, continuing to beat until the mixture is smooth and creamy. Stir in almond extract.
4. Slowly stir in sifted dry ingredients and mix well.
5. Fold in toasted nuts.
6. Divide dough into two parts and form into logs 12 by 7 inches each. Wrap in plastic wrap and chill logs for at least
7. 2 hours.
8. When ready to bake, preheat oven to 350°F.
   Place logs on an ungreased baking sheet or on parchment paper–lined baking sheet and bake 35 minutes, until light
9. brown.
   Remove from oven and allow to cool for about 10 minutes.
10. Cut each log on the diagonal into 10 or 12 pieces.
    Return to oven for 10 more minutes—5 minutes on each side. Cool on baking sheet for 5 minutes before removing to wire racks to cool. When biscotti are completely cool, dip half of each biscotti in either white or white or dark melted chocolate. Allow to set before serving.

Ingredients

- 1½ cups nuts, such as walnuts, pistachios, or almonds
- 3½ cups flour
- 1 teaspoon baking powder
- ½ cup (1 stick) butter, softened
- 1 cup sugar
- 3 eggs
- 1 teaspoon almond extract
- 4 ounces unsweetened chocolate, melted
- 4 ounces white chocolate, melted

Difficulty
Intermediate

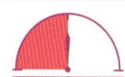

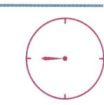

Baking Time
45 minutes

Portion
20–24 servings

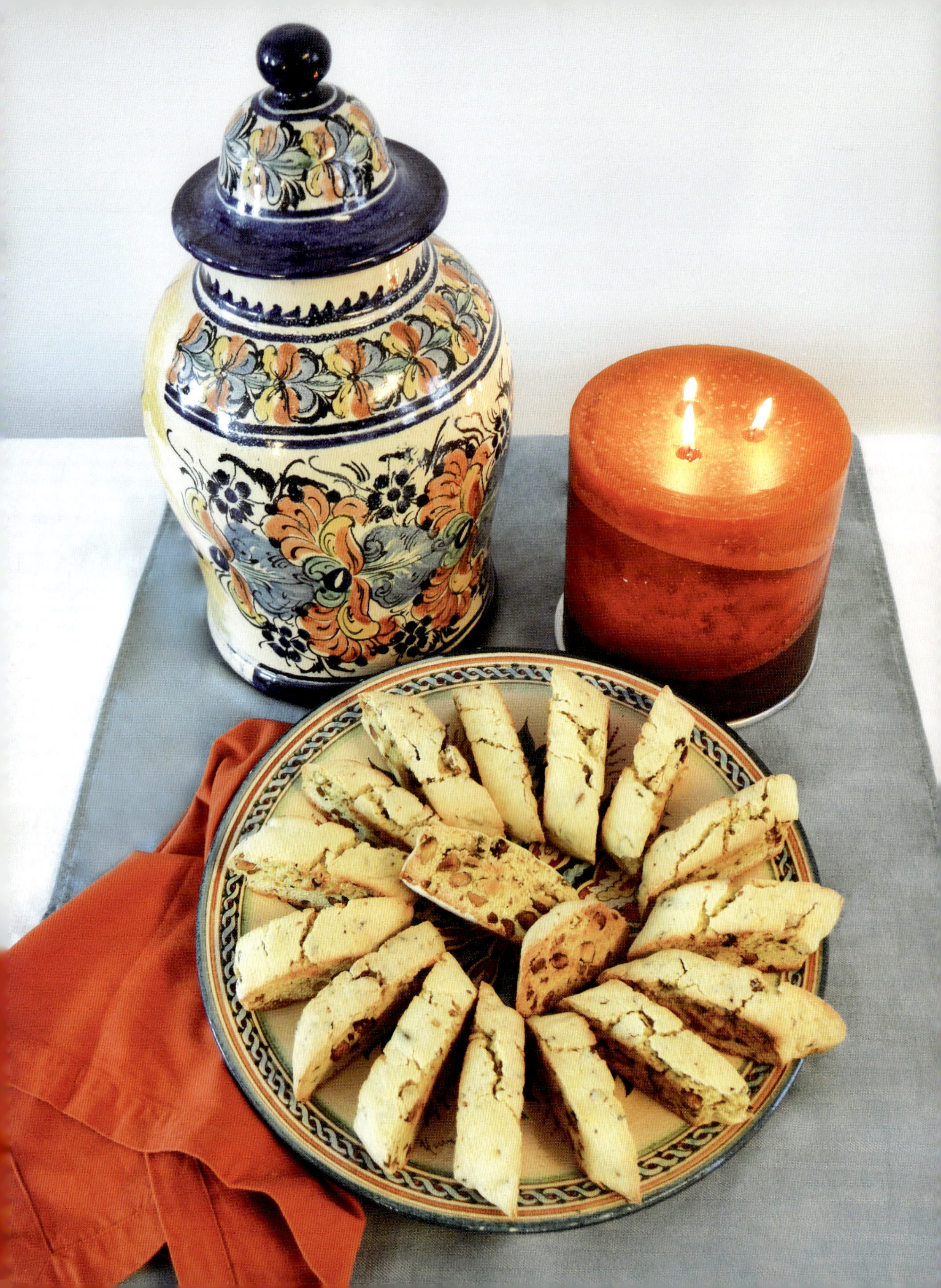

PISTACHIO BISCOTTI

These nutty, twice-baked cookies—biscotti is from the Italian bis, meaning "twice," and cotto, meaning "cooked or baked"—make a delicious afternoon treat or a light dessert.

Preparation

1. Spread the pistachios evenly on a baking sheet and bake for 8 minutes at 350°F, until lightly toasted. Set aside.
2. Sift together the flour, baking powder, and salt and set aside.
3. In a separate mixing bowl, with an electric mixer set on medium–high, beat butter until fluffy. Add white and brown sugars and eggs, one a time, continuing to beat until the mixture is smooth and creamy.
4. Stir in vanilla, then slowly add sifted dry ingredients until well combined.
5. Fold in toasted pistachios.
6. Divide dough dough into two parts and form into logs and form into two logs 14 by 6½ inches. Wrap in plastic wrap
7. and chill at least 2 hours.
8. When ready to bake, preheat oven to 350°F. Spread 3 tablespoons of sugar and the lemon zest evenly
9. on a surface. Roll each log over lemon zest and sugar. Place logs on an ungreased baking sheet and bake for 35
10. minutes. Remove from oven and slice each log on the diagonal
11. into 10 pieces each. Put biscotti back to the oven and bake 10 minutes more—5 minutes on each side—or until light brown. Cool on baking sheet for 5 minutes before removing to wire racks to cool completely.

Ingredients

- 1½ cups pistachios
- 3½ cups flour
- 1 teaspoon baking powder
- ½ teaspoon salt
- ½ cup (1 stick) butter, softened
- ¾ cup sugar
- ¼ cup brown sugar
- 3 eggs
- 1 teaspoon vanilla
- 3 tablespoons sugar, for edges
- zest of 1 lemon

Difficulty
Easy to Intermediate

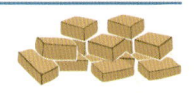

Baking Time
45 minutes

Portion
20 servings

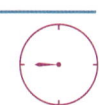

Cake Pops

- Chocolate Cake Pops -
- Vanilla Cake Pops -

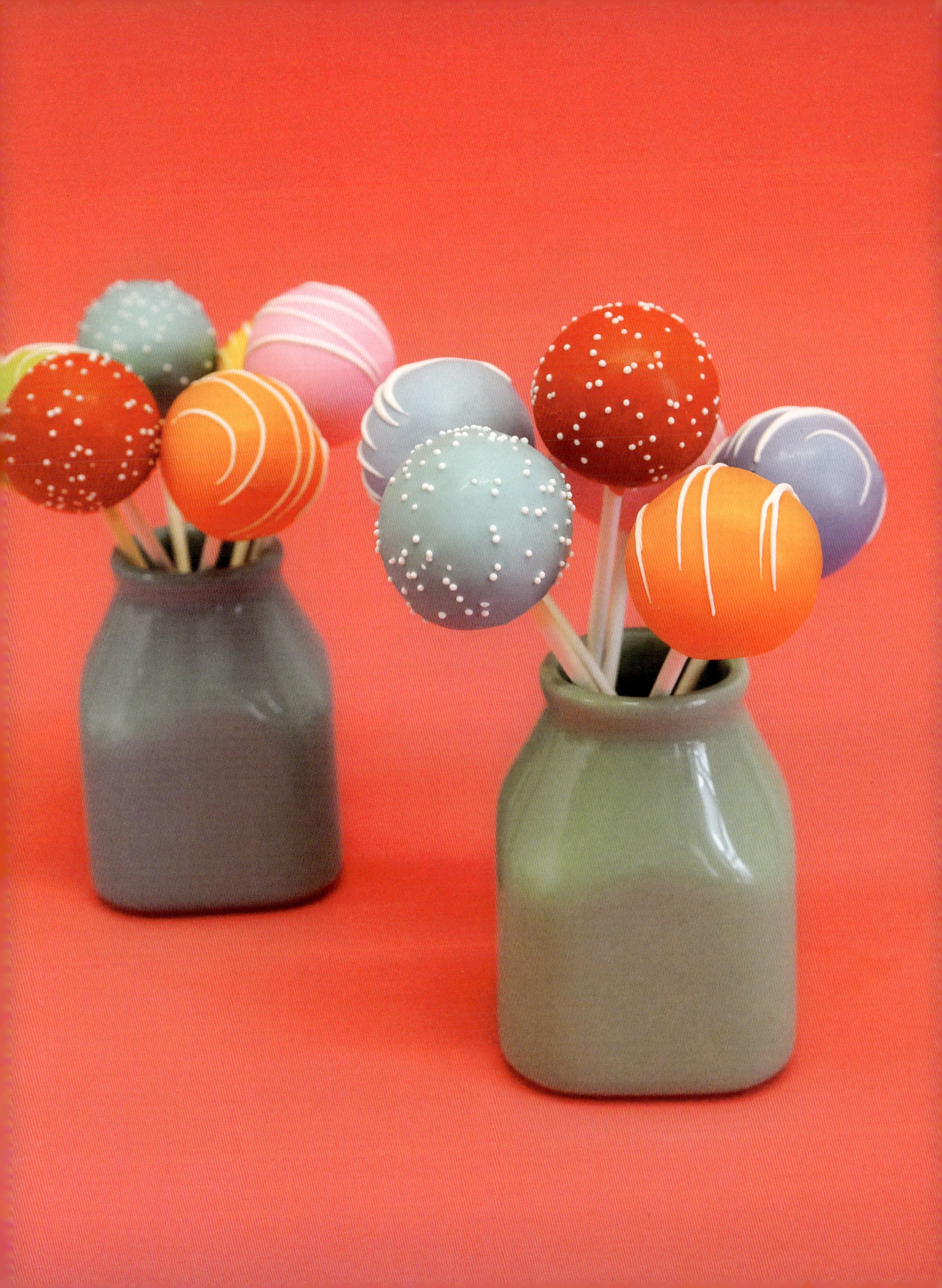

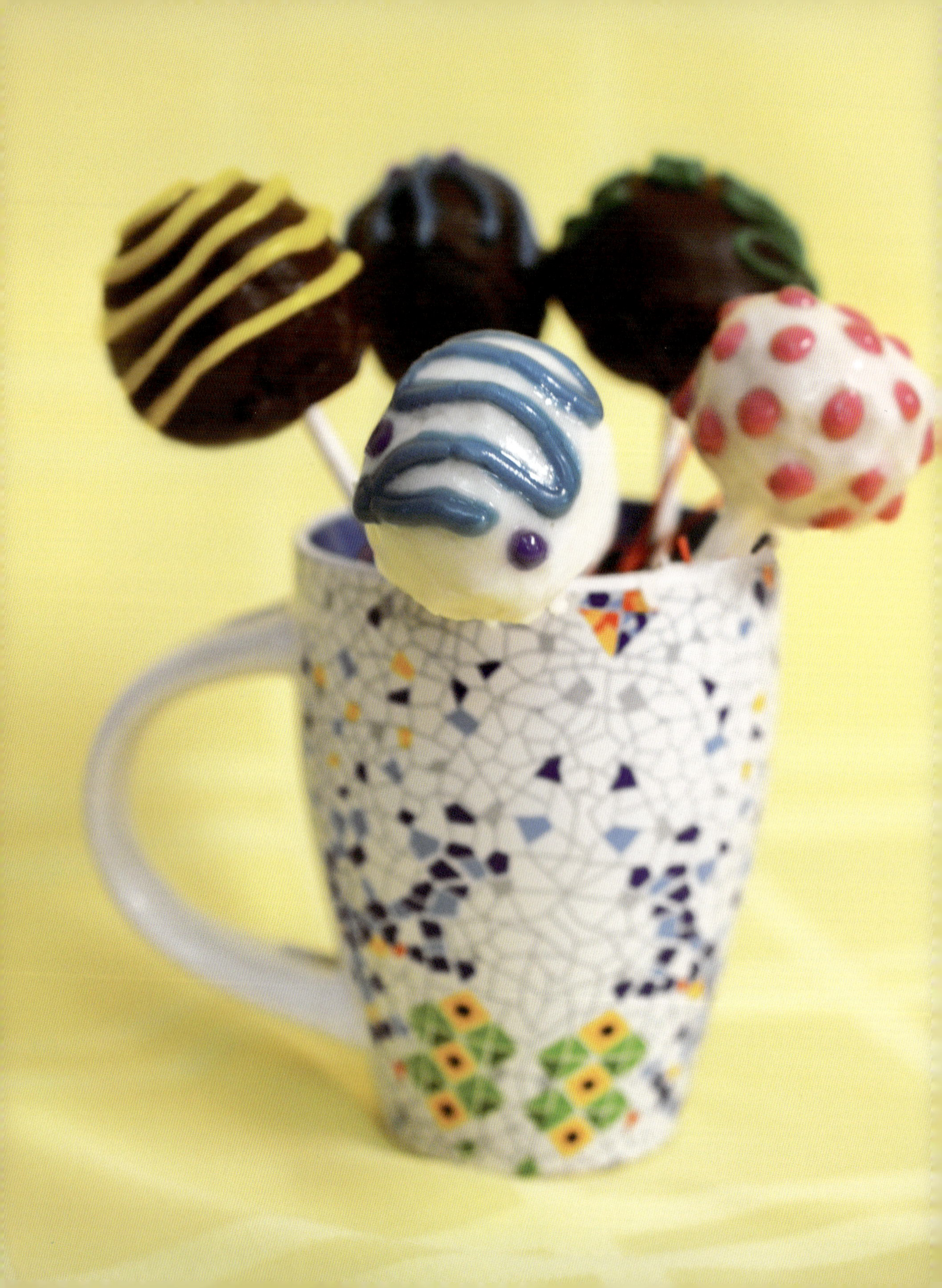

CHOCOLATE CAKE POPS

This recipe offers the ultimate in fun! Make these fantastic cake pops with the kids, then let them decorate with whimsy and feast on the fruits of their labor.

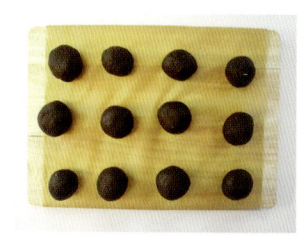

Preparation

1. Cut prepared Devil's Food Cake into small pieces (make sure it is completely cooled).
2. Put 2 cups of Creamy Chocolate Frosting in a large bowl. Add Devil's Food Cake pieces and, using your hands, blend with frosting. Work until the mix is smooth.
3. Form into balls about the size of golf balls. Place balls on a parchment paper-lined tray and freeze for 20 minutes.
4. Once Cake Pops have become firm in freezer, put a stick into each one, sealing with frosting.
5. Dip each Cake Pop in Ganache or Confectioners' Sugar Icing. Allow to set, then embellish with tinted Confectioner's Sugar Icing or other decorations

Ingredients

1 Devil's Food Cake (recipe page 25)
2 cups Creamy Chocolate Frosting (recipe page 130)
  Ganache (recipe page 132) and/or Confectioners' Sugar Icing (recipe page 123)

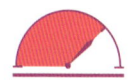

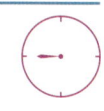

Difficulty
Advanced

Baking Time
45 minutes

Portion
24 cakepops

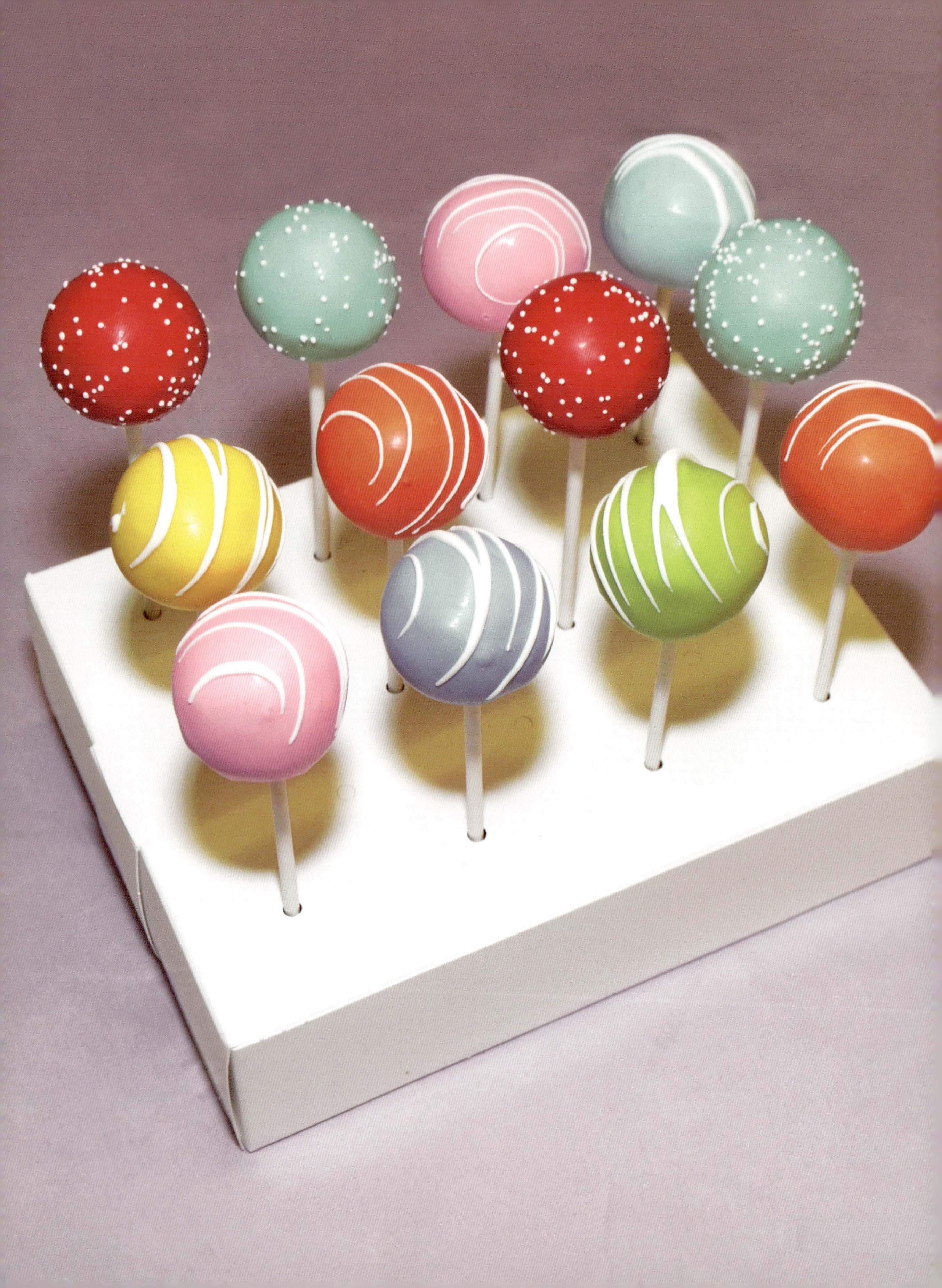

VANILLA CAKE POPS

Pretty to display and oh-so-easy to eat, these little "cake lollies" make any occasion feel like a party.

Preparation

1. Cut Golden Cake or Vanilla Cake into small pieces (make sure it is completely cooled).
2. Put 2 cup Easy Buttercream Frosting or Cream Cheese Frosting in a large bowl. Add cake pieces and, using your hands, blend with frosting. Work until the mix is smooth.
3. Form into balls about the size of golf balls. Place balls on a parchment paper-lined tray and freeze for 20 minutes.
4. Once Cake Pops have become firm in freezer, put a stick into each one, sealing with frosting.
5. Dip each Cake Pop in *Confectioners' Sugar Icing*. Then embellish with decorations as desired.

Ingredients

- Golden Cake (recipe page 31) or Vanilla Cake (recipe page 29)
- 2 cups Easy Buttercream frosting
- 4 Confectioners' Sugar Icing (recipe page 123) for decorating

Difficulty
Advanced

Baking Time
1 hour

Portion
24 cakepops

Frostings & Glazes

- Cointreau Syrup
- Vanilla Glaze
- Cream Cheese Frosting
- Whipped Cream
- Vanilla Filling Cream
- Easy Buttercream Frosting
- Fluffy White Meringue
- Confectioner's Sugar Icing
- Classic Cake Frosting
- Honey Whipped Cream
- Choco-Mint Icing
- Mocha Frosting
- Maple Frosting
- Rich Caramel Sauce
- Creamy Chocolate Frosting
- Fudge Icing
- Spreadable Chocolate Frosting
- Ganache
- German Chocolate Frosting
- Chocolate Glaze

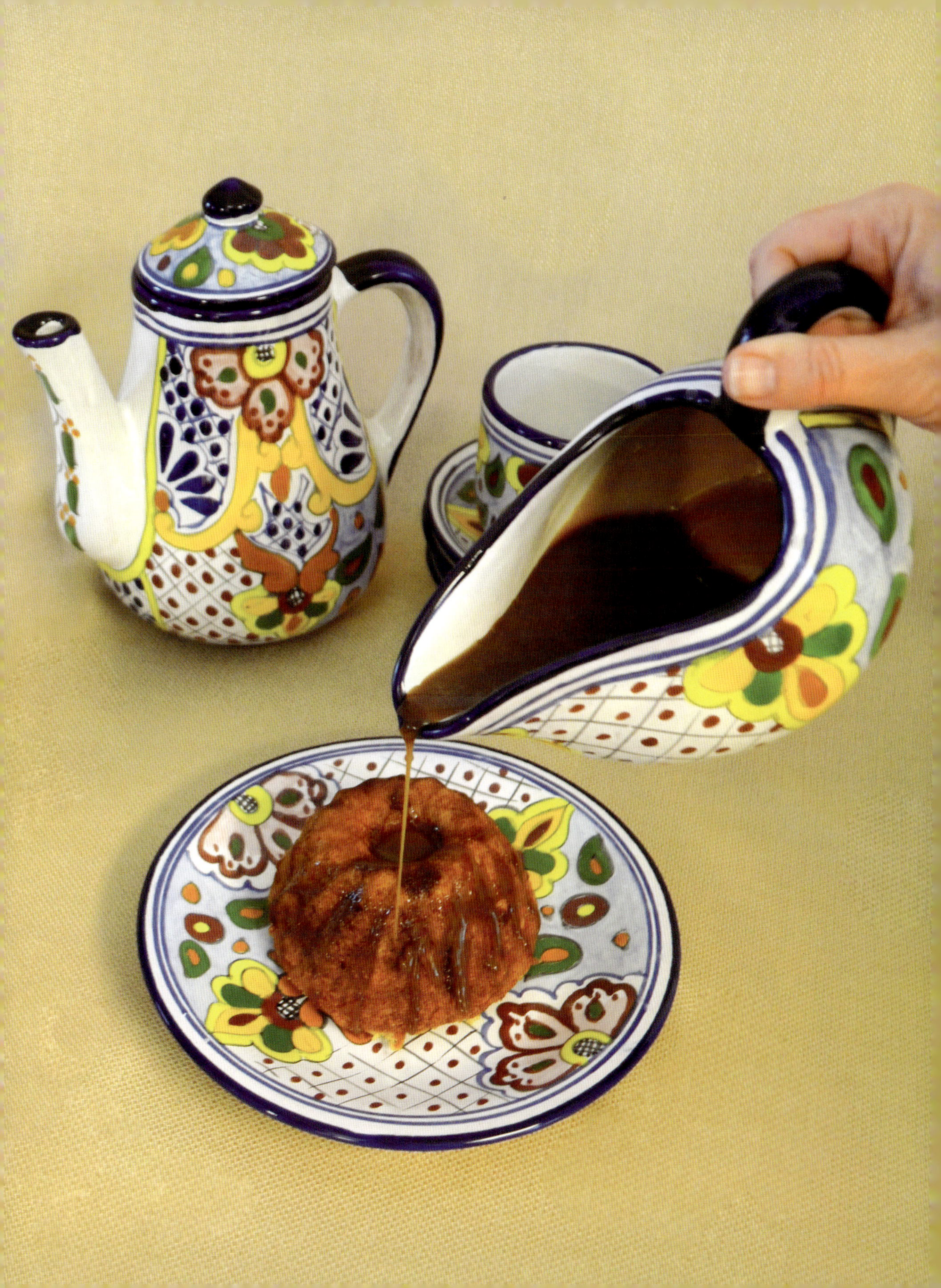

COINTREAU SYRUP

Easy to prepare, this sophisticated syrup elevates even simple cakes. Traditionally paired with orange liqueur or chocolate cakes, this syrup is the perfect topping for Orange-Nut Cake.

Ingredients

- ¾ cup sugar
- ¼ cup Cointreau or other orange liqueur
- ¼ cup fresh orange juice
- 3 tablespoons lemon juice
- ¼ teaspoon salt
- 1 teaspoon of orange zest

Preparation

Combine all ingredients in a saucepan and cook over medium heat until slightly thickened.

Difficulty
Easy

Preparation Time
10 minutes

Portion
1 cup

VANILLA GLAZE

Brown sugar and vanilla impart subtle sweetness to this basic glaze. This topping is fast and uses pantry staples—perfect for those times when you're in a hurry or don't have many ingredients on hand.

Ingredients

- 3 tablespoons butter
- 3 tablespoons brown sugar
- 3 tablespoons confectioners' sugar
- 3 tablespoons evaporated milk
- 1 teaspoon vanilla extract

Preparation

In a medium saucepan over low heat, boil all of the ingredients together for 1 minute. Remove from heat and spread or drizzle over the cake.

Difficulty
Easy

Preparation Time
10 minutes

Portion
1 cup

CREAM CHEESE FROSTING

A traditional frosting for carrot cake, Cream Cheese Frosting also makes a delectable topping for cupcakes, chocolate cake, and even cookies.

Ingredients

- 2 cups confectioners' sugar
- 8 ounces cream cheese, softened*
- ½ cup butter (1 stick), at room temperature
- 1 teaspoon vanilla extract

Preparation

1. Sift confectioners' sugar and set aside.
2. Using an electric mixer, in a separate bowl beat together the butter and cream cheese until smooth, about 3 minutes.
3. Add the powdered sugar slowly, continuing to mix. Scrape down the sides of the bowl. Add vanilla and mix until creamy.

* Do not use whipped cream cheese, it makes the frosting lumpy

Difficulty
Easy

Preparation Time
15 minutes

Portion
2 cups

WHIPPED CREAM

Light, fluffy, and pleasantly sweet, homemade whipped cream can't be beat. And it's so scrumptious, you'll never buy canned whipped topping again!

Ingredients

- 1 cup heavy cream
- ½ cup confectioners' sugar, sifted
- 1 teaspoon vanilla extract

Preparation

1. At least 2 hours before making Whipped Cream, place the mixing bowl and beater blade in the refrigerator to chill. This recipe is the exception to the rule that dairy ingredients should be room temperature before using: make sure the heavy cream is cold.
2. Beat together all of the ingredients until the consistency is thick and the cream forms soft peaks, about 4 or 5 minutes. You have about a 30-second time period where the whipped cream will change from soft peaks to lumpy and butterlike. Watch closely and stop beating before the mixture turns to sweet butter.
3. Use Whipped Cream to frost or fill cake or cupcakes. Keep refrigerated until ready to serve. Whipped Cream will keep, refrigerated, 1 to 2 days.

Difficulty
Intermediate

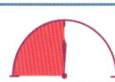

Preparation Time
2.5 hours

Portion
2 cups

VANILLA FILLING CREAM

Ideal for layering between cakes or cookies, this airy filling can be flavored with other essences as well—experiment with different extracts and liqueurs to complement your favorite cakes.

Ingredients

- 1 cup milk
- 5 tablespoons sugar
- 3 egg yolks
- 3 tablespoons cornstarch
- 1 teaspoon butter, softened
- 2 tablespoons water
- 1 teaspoon vanilla extract or cognac

Preparation

1. In a saucepan over medium heat, heat milk and 2 tablespoons of the sugar until sugar is dissolved and milk is boiling. Remove from heat and set aside.
2. In a bowl, whisk together egg yolks and remaining 3 tablespoons of sugar until well combined. Stir into the saucepan with milk mixture and continue to whisk. Return to heat.
3. In a small bowl, whisk cornstarch with 2 tablespoons water. Add cornstarch mixture to the saucepan and continue to whisk until thickened. Remove from heat. Add butter and vanilla and whisk until well blended.
4. Use to fill cakes. If not using immediately, store in a tightly
5. covered container in the refrigerator for 2 to 3 days. If the filling is refrigerated, whisk lightly to restore.

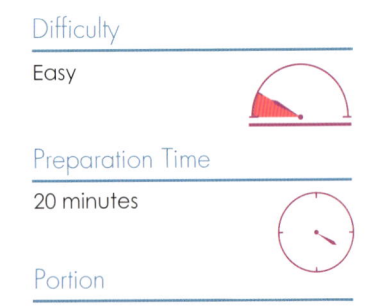

Difficulty
Easy

Preparation Time
20 minutes

Portion
1 cup

EASY BUTTERCREAM FROSTING

The most popular frosting among baking enthusiasts, buttercream is both delicious and easy to spread—it's ideal for piping borders and flowers too, if you like to decorate with flair.

Ingredients

- ½ cup butter (1 stick), softened
- 3 cups confectioners' sugar, sifted
- 3 tablespoons heavy cream
- 1 teaspoon vanilla extract
- pinch of salt

Preparation

1. In a large bowl, cream the butter with an electric mixer until very soft and light, about 3 minutes.
2. Add the sifted sugar to the butter, and stir in the heavy cream, vanilla, and salt. Beat until smooth and fluffy, about 3 to 5 minutes.
3. Use immediately or seal in an airtight container and refrigerate. The frosting will keep for about one week. Before using, whisk the frosting until consistency is soft and fluffy.

Difficulty
Easy

Preparation Time
10 minutes

Portion
1 cup

FLUFFY WHITE MERINGUE

This meringue is made using the Italian method of combining hot sugar syrup with whipped egg whites, creating a softer and more stable topping.

Ingredients

- ½ cup water
- 1 cup sugar
- 3 egg whites

Preparation

1. In a small saucepan, bring the water and sugar to a low boil and cook until sugar is dissolved and mixture turns a light caramel color. You'll know it's ready when you can move a spatula across the bottom of the pan. Remove from heat.
   While the syrup is cooking, separate the eggs. Set aside.
2. In a large bowl, with an electric mixer on high speed, beat
3. the egg whites together until they stiffen. Reduce mixer speed to low and add the hot syrup little by little, beating until meringue holds its shape, about 3 to 5 minutes.
   Use immediately, spreading or piping over cake or
4. cupcakes.

Difficulty
Intermediate

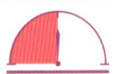

Preparation Time
20 minutes

Portion
2 cups

CONFECTIONERS' SUGAR ICING

This easy-to-make white or colored icing is essential and can be used for icings, piping, and fillings, or for dipping almost any cookie or cupcake.

Ingredients

- 1 cup confectioners' sugar
- 1 tablespoon milk

Optional:
- 1 teaspoon of cocoa

Preparation

1. Whisk together the confectioners' sugar and milk until smooth.
2. In a medium bowl, separate 1/2 a cup of icing and add 2 drops of your favorite food coloring. Mix thoroughly and add more to darken color, if desired.
3. Continue with the remaining icing and colors of your choice.
4. Add 1 teaspoon of cocoa to make chocolate flavored icing, add milk as necessary.

Difficulty
Easy

Preparation Time
10 minutes

Portion
1 cup

CLASSIC CAKE FROSTING

This frosting has been gracing homemade cakes for generations. Its simple ingredients and straightforward steps make this recipe one to keep close at hand!

Ingredients

- 3 egg whites
- 1 cup sugar
- ⅓ cup light corn syrup

Preparation

1. Separate the eggs, set aside yolks for another use.
2. In a metal or other heatproof mixing bowl, mix together egg whites, sugar, and corn syrup.
3. Place heatproof mixing bowl over a large saucepan of simmering water and whisk constantly until sugar is dissolved, about 2 to 3 minutes.
4. Remove from heat and beat on high with an electric mixer or in a stand mixer until peaks form, about 5 to 7 minutes. Use immediately.

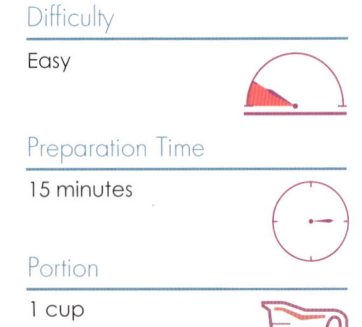

Difficulty

Easy

Preparation Time

15 minutes

Portion

1 cup

HONEY WHIPPED CREAM

A dollop of honey gives whipped cream a sweetly floral flavor. It's the perfect topping for Chai Cupcakes, and pairs well with any fruit dessert or with a dish of fresh fruit or ice cream.

Ingredients

- 1 cup heavy cream
- 2 tablespoons honey

Preparation

In a chilled bowl, using a whisk or an electric mixer, whip together heavy cream and honey until thickened, 3 to 5 minutes.

Difficulty
Easy

Preparation Time
10 minutes

Portion
2 cups

CHOCO-MINT ICING

This flavorful syrup gets a triple dose of orange—from liqueur, fresh juice, and zest. Use it as a glaze for cakes or as a sophisticated topping for ice cream.

Ingredients

- ⅓ cup butter, softened
- ⅓ cup cocoa
- 2 cups contectioners' sugar, sifted
- 3 tablespoons heavy cream
- 1 teaspoon vanilla extract or 1/2 teaspoon peppermint extract
- ¼ cup crushed peppermint candies

Preparation

1. Mix together butter and cocoa, then stir in sifted confectioners' sugar, heavy cream, and vanilla.
2. Mix until smooth. Spread icing on brownies and sprinkle with crushed peppermint candies.

Difficulty
Easy-Intermediate

Preparation Time
10 minutes

Portion
1 cup

MOCHA FROSTING

Espresso powder lends this dreamy frosting its undeniable coffee flavor. Pair it with yellow or chocolate cakes for an interesting variation on the classics.

Preparation

1. Mix the espresso powder into hot water until dissolved. Add vanilla and set aside.
2. Using an electric mixer, beat the butter on medium speed until creamy, about 5 minutes, stopping once to scrape the sides of the bowl.
3. Reduce the speed to low and add the confectioners' sugar, adding a little bit at a time. Turn off mixer and scrape the sides of the bowl as necessary. Once all the sugar is incorporated, increase the speed to medium-high and whip until fluffy, about 1 to 2 minutes.
4. Add the espresso and vanilla mixture to the whipped frosting and beat until well combined. Use to fill or frost cake or cupcakes. Refrigerate until ready to serve. The frosting will keep, refrigerated, 2 to 3 days.

Ingredients

- 4 teaspoons instant espresso powder
- ¼ cup hot water
- 1½ teaspoon vanilla extract
- 1 cup butter (2 sticks), softened
- 2½ cups confectioners' sugar, sifted

Difficulty
Easy-Intermediate

Preparation Time
10 minutes

Portion
2 cups

MAPLE FROSTING

As the leaves change colors, our mouths water for the tastes of autumn. This cream cheese–based frosting offers just the right touch of sweet maple.

Ingredients

- 8 ounces cream cheese, softened
- ¾ cup (1 1/2 sticks) unsalted butter, softened
- ½ teaspoon maple extract
- ¾ cup packed dark brown sugar
- 2 cups confectioners' sugar, sifted

Preparation

1. Beat cream cheese with butter until creamy. Stir in maple extract.
2. Beat in brown sugar and confectioners' sugar until frosting is fluffy. Store in an airtight container in the refrigerator for up to 2 weeks.

Difficulty
Easy

Preparation Time
15 minutes

Portion
2 cups

RICH CARAMEL SAUCE

Rich and gooey, this caramel sauce couldn't be easier—and the final product couldn't be more delicious.

Preparation

1. Spread granulated sugar evenly over bottom of a large saucepan or skillet. Heat the sugar on medium–low. Edges will begin to cook first; push them toward the middle with a heatproof spatula so the sugar does not burn. If lumps appear, turn heat down slightly and slowly stir.
2. Continue stirring as you cook the sugar to a deep amber color; do not allow it to burn. Remove the sugar from the heat and let cool for a couple of minutes.
3. Add ½ cup of boiling water and ½ cup maple syrup and return to the heat until the sauce thickens.
4. Finish the sauce by melting ¾ cup butter and adding sifted confectioners' sugar to it slowly. Add the Caramel from step 3 and mix until well combined.
5. Pour Rich Caramel Sauce over the cake edge so that it drips decoratively down the sides.

Ingredients

- 1 cup sugar
- ½ cup boiling water
- ½ teaspoon maple syrup
- ¾ cup butter
- 1 cup confectioners' sugar, sifted

Difficulty
Intermediate

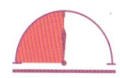

Preparation Time
20 minutes

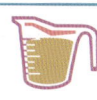

Portion
2 cups

CREAMY CHOCOLATE FROSTING

Creamy and dreamy, this frosting is a versatile star, perfect for any cake or cupcake that needs a rich, chocolaty topping.

Ingredients

- 6 ounces unsweetened chocolate
- 1 cup butter (2 sticks), softened
- 2 cups confectioners' sugar, sifted
- 1 teaspoon vanilla extract

Preparation

1. Break up the squares of chocolate. In a small saucepan, melt the chocolate over a double boiler or over low heat. Set aside.
2. In an electric mixer set on low, beat the butter until creamy, about 4 to 5 minutes.
3. Add the sifted confectioners' sugar to the creamed butter, beating until sugar is mixed in evenly.
4. Add the melted chocolate to the mixture and continue to mix on low until completely blended. Add vanilla and mix until well blended.
5. Use immediately or refrigerate in an airtight container for up to 2 weeks.

Difficulty
Easy- intermediate

Preparation Time
10 minutes

Portion
1 cup

FUDGE ICING

Gooey and chocolate-y, Fudge Icing adds the perfect sweet boost to nearly any dessert! Add a bright note of peppermint to your desserts with this lush chocolate-mint icing. It's an especially lovely topping for brownies at Christmas time.

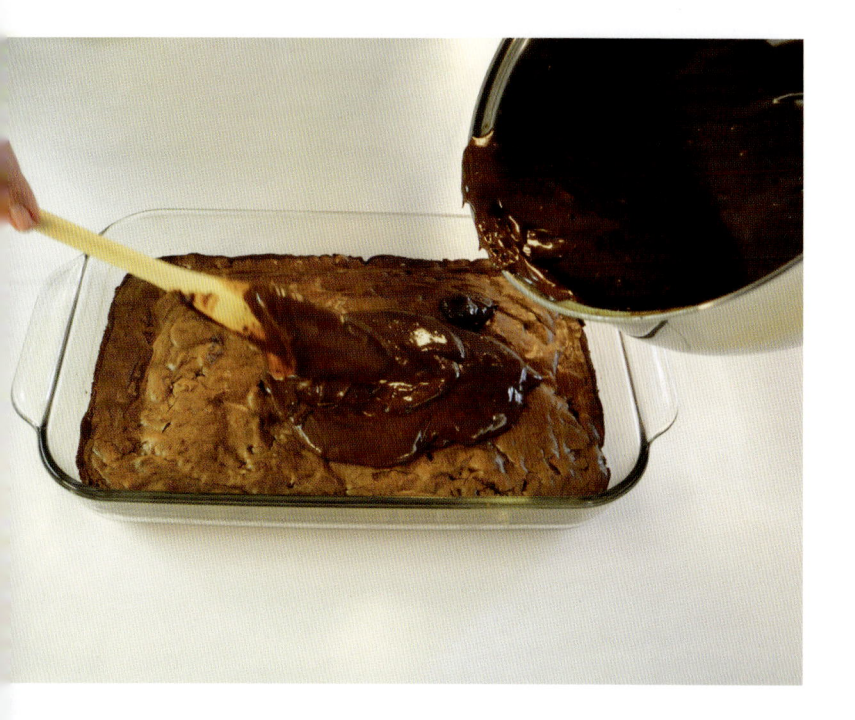

Ingredients

- 1 14-ounce can sweetened condensed milk
- 2 ounces unsweetened chocolate
- 2 tablespoons water
- 1 tablespoon butter

Preparation

Combine all ingredients in a saucepan and heat on medium-low. Stir constantly until the mixture begins to boil. Continue boiling for about 8 minutes, stirring regularly. The icing is ready when the bottom of the pot shows when you stir the mixture aside.

Difficulty
Easy

Preparation Time
15 minutes

Portion
2 cups

SPREADABLE CHOCOLATE FROSTING

This chocolate frosting goes on easy—it's perfect for kids to use, as they won't have to worry about getting cake crumbs into the icing.

Ingredients

- 2 ounces unsweetened chocolate
- 1 13.5-ounce can sweetened condensed milk
- 1 12-ounce can evaporated milk
- 1 tablespoon butter
- 1 teaspoon vanilla extract

Preparation

Place all of the ingredients in a small saucepan over medium–low heat. Bring to a low boil and stir constantly for 5 to 8 minutes, until the ingredients thicken and the consistency is of spreadable frosting. Use immediately.

Difficulty
Easy

Preparation Time
20 minutes

Portion
2 cups

GANACHE

Perfect as a glaze, this versatile ganache can also be gently whipped and used as a frosting.

Ingredients

- 8 ounces semisweet chocolate
- 8 ounces heavy cream
- 1 tablespoon butter

Preparation

1. Using a serrated knife, finely chop the chocolate into pieces.
2. In a saucepan, heat cream and butter over medium-high heat, stirring constantly until it just comes to a boil.
3. Pour the cream and butter over the chocolate and stir until it is smooth and all the chocolate has melted, about two minutes. Allow to cool, then use as a glaze for cakes and cupcakes or make a whipped frosting by allowing to cool to room temperature, stirring occasionally, then mixing with electric mixer until the frosting is fluffy. Store ganache in the refrigerator, tightly covered, for up to two weeks.

Difficulty
Intermediate

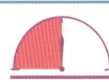

Preparation Time
30 minutes

Portion
2 cups

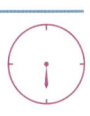

GERMAN CHOCOLATE FROSTING

Divinely sweet, this frosting is chock-full of coconut and pecans. It's so yummy, you're apt to forget there's cake to be eaten beneath it!

Ingredients

- 4 egg yolks
- 1 12 ounce can evaporated milk
- ¾ cup granulated white sugar
- ¼ cup brown sugar
- ½ cup butter (1 stick)
- 2 cups shredded coconut
- 1 cup pecans, halved

Preparation

1. Beat egg yolks with a fork until frothy. Set aside.
2. In a saucepan, combine evaporated milk, white sugar, brown sugar, and butter, and heat on medium-low. Bring to a boil, stirring constantly, about 8 minutes.
3. Remove from heat and add egg yolks a little at a time, stirring constantly. Return to heat until mixture is thickening, for up to 5 minutes.
4. Stir in coconut and pecans and set frosting aside until thickened, about 8 to 10 minutes. Use immediately.

Difficulty
Intermediate

Preparation Time
30 minutes

Portion
2

CHOCOLATE GLAZE

This simple glaze turns any cakes or cookie into a chocolate-lover's delight!

Ingredients

- 1   14-ounce can sweetened condensed milk
- 1   tablespoon water
- 4   ounces unsweetened chocolate
- 1   pinch salt
- 1   teaspoon butter
- 1   teaspoon vanilla extract

Preparation

1. In a saucepan over medium–low heat combine the condensed milk, water, chocolate, and salt. Cook, stirring constantly to prevent sticking, until the sauce is a thick, caramel consistency, about 10 to 12 minutes.
2. Add vanilla and butter, and stir to blend. Use immediately.

Difficulty
Easy

Preparation Time
20 minutes

Portion
2 cups

ABOUT THE AUTHOR

Special thanks:

To my mom, who gave me all the skills I needed to start a new career. And to my dad, who told me that to be happy I needed to work at what I really love.

To my daughters, who always share with me new recipes and our traditions.

To my husband, for providing me with the opportunity to study and do what I love. And for being my best taster.

To my team, Carol, Karen, and Elizabeth, who make this project my dream come true.

Patricia Cartin Fernandez was born and raised in San Jose, Costa Rica. She graduated with a degree in international business from the University of Costa Rica and the International University of the Americas in Costa Rica. For more than fifteen years, she served as an executive for different companies in Costa Rica, as well as becoming executive director of the Junior Achievement Progam. She worked as a development manager for new projects involving debit cards for an international bank, and was also manager of project implementation in payroll outsourcing and temporary hires for various companies.

When she moved to the United States after her husband's corporate transfer, she decided to follow her dreams and explore her passion for baking and cooking. From the age of six, Patricia was captivated by the aromas and flavors that emerged from the family kitchen, and she had always counted the culinary arts as a favorite hobby. But it was her move to America that sparked her desire to study cooking professionally and radically change her career. She graduated from the prestigious French Culinary School in Manhattan (ICC), with a concentration in cake techniques and design.

Patricia began her own thriving business teaching baking and cooking from her home. Because she is passionate about culinary arts, she is dedicated to learning new recipes and techniques—and she can regularly be found taking courses in addition to teaching them. When visiting Costa Rica, she meets with a group of chefs who cook together and exchange recipes. Patricia loves learning from other chefs and sharing her own knowledge because: "In the kitchen there are no secrets!"

Appendix

Baking Tips and Tricks

- Most ovens take twenty to thirty minutes to preheat fully. Factor in this time in when planning your baking project.

- Using a different pan size or using glass instead of metal will change the baking time and alter the results. Bright metal pans work best. If you want to experiment with a different type of pan, be sure to watch your cake closely and begin testing for doneness ten minutes before the specified bake time is up.

- Cake batter should fill the pan at least halfway and not more than two thirds, unless the recipe specifies otherwise.

- Bake your cake in the middle of the oven, if possible. Rotate the pans in the oven to ensure even baking, but wait til about two thirds of the way into baking time to make sure the cake has set. If you are baking more than one cake or pan of cupcakes or cookies, swap them on the shelves partway through the baking time. If you have a baking stone in your oven, place the pans in the middle.

- Cooling your cakes upside-down will flatten out the tops, and make it easier to stack them if you are making a layer cake.

- Wait until cakes are completely cool before frosting. Glazes and syrups are sometimes drizzled over warm baked goods, however, so they are absorbed into the cake.

- Adjusting cookie baking time will change the texture of your cookies. A bit less time will make chewy cookies, while a little time added to the clock produces crispier cookies.

- Make sure cookies are completely cool before storing them; otherwise, they will get soggy.

- Don't store different types of cookies in the same container; the different moisture levels in the cookies will make some soggy and others taste stale.

- Many cakes and cookies can be successfully frozen. Wrap unfrosted cakes tightly in plastic wrap. Freeze frosted cakes by setting the cake, unwrapped, in the freezer on a foil-lined baking sheet. Once the cake has frozen hard, wrap it in plastic wrap and return to the freezer. Cookies can be layered in an airtight container lined with waxed paper or plastic wrap. Note that if frosted cookies are layered, the icing may not survive the freezing well—it often causes cookies to stick together or to the wrap.

Metric Conversions

(Conversions are approximate)

Measurements

Imperial	Metric
¼ teaspoon	1 ml
½ teaspoon	2 ml
1 teaspoon	5 ml
1 tablespoon	15 ml
2 tablespoons	25 ml
3 tablespoons	50 ml
¼ cup	50 ml
⅓ cup	75 ml
½ cup	125 ml
⅔ cup	150 ml
¾ cup	175 ml
1 cup	250 ml

Temperature

Farenheit	Celsius
32°	0°
212°	100°
250°	121°
275°	140°
300°	150°
325°	160°
350°	180°
375°	190°
400°	200°
425°	220°
450°	230°
475°	240°

Yields for Common Baking Ingredients

(Yields are approximate)

Ingredient	The recipe calls for:	You will need:
Butter	1 cup	2 sticks
Chocolate chips	1 cup	6 ounces
Cream Cheese	1 cup	8 ounces
Dates	2½ cups, pitted	1 pound
Flour, all-purpose	3½ cups	1 pound
Honey	1 cup	12 ounces
Raisins	1 cup	5 ounces
Sugar, granulated	2 cups	1 pound
Sugar, powdered	4 cups	1 pound
Walnuts	4 cups	1 pound

Baking Resources

Following is a selected list of online suppliers that carry baking supplies and kitchen equipment and/or ingredients. A quick search will yield hundreds of others, likely including some specialty baking shops in your area.

- Broadway Panhandler
  Bakeware and kitchen equipment
  www.broadwaypanhandler.com

- Chicago Metallic
  Bakeware and specialty pans
  www.chicagometallicbakeware.com

- Fishs Eddy
  Purveyors of dinnerware, glassware, & serveware.
  www.fishseddy.com

- KitchenKrafts
  Specialty pans, cake decorating supplies, food colorings
  www.kitchenkrafts.com

- Michaels
  Cake decorating tools and supplies
  www.michaels.com

- ShopBakersNook.com
  Baking and cake decorating supplies
  www.shopbakersnook.com

- US Cake Supply
  Specialty bakeware and decorating tools
  www.uscakesupply.com

- Wilton
  Baking equipment, including shaped cake pans and pastry bags and tips
  www.wilton.com

SPECIAL THANKS TO FISHS EDDY
A great place for beautiful tabletop supplies

INDEX

A
Allspice, 91
Apple Cake, 46–47
Apricot Upside-Down Cake, 44–45

B
Bars, cooky
Brownie Bars with Fudge Icing, 98–99
Cinnamon and Coffee Bars, 96–97
Classic Chocolate Brownie, 101
Coconut-Toffee Bars, 100
Cranberry-Orange Shortbreads, 102–103
    easy level, 97, 99, 101
    intermediate level, 100, 103
    log, 103
Biscotti
    Chocolate-Dipped Biscotti, 104–105
    intermediate level, 105, 107
    Pistachio Biscotti, 106–107
Black and White Sugar Cookies, 88–89
Brownie Bars with Fudge Icing, 98–99
Brownie Crinkles, 68
Butter, 8
Butter Cookies, 86–87
Buttercream Frosting, 31, 35, 43, 59, 93, 113, 121
Buttermilk, 59, 63, 79

C
Cake Pops, 108–113
Chocolate Cake Pops, 110–111
    difficult level, 41, 111, 113
    Vanilla Cake Pops, 112–113
Cakes, 22–49
    Apple Cake, 46–47
    Apricot Upside-Down Cake, 44–45
    baking, 14
    Caramel Cake, 38–39
    Carrot Cake with Cream Cheese Frosting, 40–41
    Chocolate Almond Mini Cakes, 26–27
    Chocolate Chip Cake, 28
    Coconut Layer Cake, 34–35
    cutting, 17
    Devil's Food Cake, 24–25, 111
    easy level, 25, 27, 28, 29, 31, 37, 43, 49
    German Chocolate Coconut Layer Cake, 36–37
    Golden Cake with Buttercream and Walnuts, 30–31
    icing, 16, 17
    intermediate level, 33, 35, 39, 41, 45, 47
    layer, 24–25, 31, 35, 41
    Orange-Chocolate Cupcakes, 54–55
    Orange-Nut Cake with Cointreau Syrup, 48–49
    pound cake, 31
    Rich Yellow Cake, 113
    Sponge Cake with Strawberries and Whipped Cream, 32–33
    unmolding, 14
    Vanilla Cake with Mocha Icing, 29
Cake stands, 20
Caramel Cake, 38–39
Carrot Cake with Cream Cheese Frosting, 40–41
Carrots, 41
Chai Cupcakes, 62–63
Chocolate
    bittersweet, 123
    chips, 28, 69, 71
    cocoa, 53, 59, 67, 69, 79, 99, 101
    melting, 12–13
    semisweet, 9, 27, 71, 123, 133
    sweet, 37
    unsweetened, 9, 25, 27, 59, 67, 68, 77, 101, 105, 130, 131, 132, 135
    white, 69, 71, 105
Chocolate Almond Mini Cakes, 26–27
Chocolate Cake Pops, 110–111
Chocolate Chip Cake, 28
Chocolate-Dipped Biscotti, 104–105
Chocolate Ganache, 53, 89, 133
Chocolate Glaze, 135
Chocolate Thumbprint Cookies with Strawberry Jelly, 66–67
Choco-Mint Icing, 101, 118

Cinnamon, 41, 47, 91, 97
Cinnamon and Coffee Bars, 96–97
Classic Cake Frosting, 124
Classic Chocolate Brownie, 101
Cloves, 91
Coconut, 35, 37, 100, 134
Coconut Layer Cake, 34–35
Coconut-Toffee Bars, 100
Coconut-Toffee Topping, 100
Coffee, 97
    espresso, 127
Cointreau, 43, 49
Cointreau Syrup, 116
Confectioners' Sugar Icing, 87, 89, 91, 123
Cookies, 64–93
    baking, 14
    balls, 67, 68, 69, 75, 77, 87, 89
    Black and White Sugar Cookies, 88–89
    Brownie Crinkles, 68
    Butter Cookies, 86–87
    Chocolate Thumbprint Cookies with Strawberry Jelly, 66–67
    cutout, 80–81, 83, 85, 87, 91, 93
    Delicate Almond Cookies, 80–81
    drop, 71, 73, 76
    easy level, 67, 69, 71, 73, 75, 77, 81, 83, 91
    Ebony and Ivory Spirals and Marbles, 78–79
    filled, 85
    Gingerbread Cookies, 90–91
    intermediate level, 79, 85, 87, 89, 93
    Linzer Heart with Rasberry Jam, 84–85
    log, 78–79
    Oatmeal Raisin Cookies, 72–73
    rolled, 78–79
    Sour Cream Cookies, 76
    Spicy Dark Chocolate Cookies, 77
    Sugar Cookie Cream Sandwiches, 92–93
    Zesty Lemon Stars, 82–83
    Cranberries, 11, 103
    Cranberry-Orange Shortbreads, 102–103

Cream
    cheese, 41, 113, 126, 128
    filling, 35, 120
    heavy, 121, 133
    honey whipped, 63, 125
    sour, 57, 76
    whipped, 33, 119, 125
Cream Cheese Frosting, 41, 113, 126
Creamy Chocolate Frosting, 55, 130
Cupcakes, 50–63
    Chai Cupcakes, 62–63
    Cupcakes with Sour Cream and Raisins, 56–57
    easy level, 53, 57, 59, 61, 63
    icing, 18
    intermediate level, 55
    Red Velvet Cupcakes, 58–59
    Super-Rich Chocolate Cupcakes, 52–53
    Vanilla Cupcakes, 60–61
    Cupcakes with Sour Cream and Raisins, 56–57

D
Decorating
    cakes, 16, 17
    cookies, 19
    cupcakes, 19
Devil's Food Cake, 24–25, 111

E
Ebony and Ivory Spirals and Marbles, 78–79
Eggs, 8, 10–11
Equipment, baking, 14, 15, 17
Extracts and flavorings
    almond, 27, 105
    maple, 128
    orange liqueur, 43
    peppermint
    vanilla, 25, 29, 31, 35, 39, 43, 45, 47, 49, 53, 55, 59, 61, 67, 69, 71, 73, 87, 89, 93, 103, 107, 117, 119, 120, 126, 127, 130, 132

F

Flavorings. See Extracts and flavorings
Flour, 8
Fluffy White Meringue, 122
Frostings and Icings
    Buttercream Frosting, 31, 35, 43, 59, 93, 113, 121
    Chocolate Ganache, 53, 89, 133
    Choco-Mint Icing, 101, 118
    Classic Cake Frosting, 124
    Coconut-Toffee Topping, 100
    coloring, 19
    Confectioners' Sugar Icing, 87, 89, 91, 123
    Cream Cheese Frosting, 41, 113, 126
    Creamy Chocolate Frosting, 55, 111, 130
    easy level, 120, 121, 123, 126, 128, 130, 131, 132
    Fluffy White Meringue, 122
    Fudge Icing, 99, 131
    German Chocolate Frosting, 37, 134
    Honey Whipped Cream, 63
    intermediate level, 122, 124, 127, 133, 134
    Maple Frosting, 128
    Mocha Frosting, 127
    Mocha Icing, 29
    piping tips, 17
    Spreadable Chocolate Frosting, 132
    Vanilla Filling Cream, 120
Fruits
    apples, 47
    apricot, 43, 45
    cranberries, 11, 103
    grapes, 43
    lemons, 83, 116
    raisins, 11, 41, 49, 57, 73, 97
    raspberry, 85
    strawberries
Fudge Icing, 99, 131

G

German Chocolate Coconut Layer Cake, 36–37
German Chocolate Frosting, 37, 134
Ginger, 77
    candied, 77, 91
    ground, 91
Gingerbread Cookies, 90–91
Glazes. See also Frostings and Icings
    Chocolate Glaze, 25, 135
    easy level, 117, 135
    Vanilla Glaze, 47, 117
Golden Cake with Buttercream and Walnuts, 30–31
Green Grapes Cake, 42–43

H

Honey, 63
Honey Whipped Cream, 63, 125

I

Ingredients
    butter, 8
    dry, 8
    eggs, 8, 10–11
    Flour, 8
    folding, 12
    leavening, 9
    measuring, 10
    milk, 8
    mixing, 11
    salt, 9

J

Jellies and jams
    apricot, 43
    rasberry, 85
    strawberry, 67

L

Lemon, 83
    juice, 76, 116
    zest, 107
Linzer Hearts with Raspberry Jam, 84–85

M

Maple Frosting, 128
Milk, 8
    buttermilk, 59, 63, 79
    condensed, 123, 131, 132, 135
    evaporated, 117, 132
Mixed-Chip Cookies, 70–71
Mocha Frosting, 127

Mocha Icing, 29
Molasses, 91

N
Nutmeg, 41, 47
Nuts, 28, 49, 105
    almonds, 27, 67, 81, 100
    pecans, 37, 39, 134
    pistachios, 107
    walnuts, 31, 39, 41, 47, 71, 97, 99, 123

O
Oatmeal Raisin Cookies, 72–73
Orange
    juice, 49, 57, 116
    peel, 55, 103
    zest, 116
Orange-Chocolate Cupcakes, 54–55
Orange-Nut Cake with Cointreau Syrup, 48–49

P
Pastry bags, 18
Peanut Butter Cookies, 74–75
Peppermint candies
Pistachio Biscotti, 106–107
Pumpkin pie spice, 77, 103

R
Raisins, 11, 41, 49, 57, 73, 97
Red Velvet Cupcakes, 58–59
Rich Caramel Sauce, 27, 39, 129
Rich Yellow Cake, 113

S
Salt, 9
Sauces
    intermediate level, 129
    Rich Caramel Sauce, 27, 39, 129
Shortbreads
    Cranberry-Orange Shortbreads, 102–103
Sour Cream Cookies, 76
Spices
    allspice, 91
    cinnamon, 41, 47, 91, 97
    cloves, 91
    ginger, 77, 91
    nutmeg, 41, 47
    pumpkin pie, 77, 103
Spicy Dark Chocolate Cookies, 77
Sponge Cake with Strawberries and Whipped Cream, 32–33
Spreadable Chocolate Frosting, 132
Strawberries, 33
Sugar, 8
    brown, 8, 41, 45, 63, 75, 91, 97, 117, 128, 134
    confectioners', 8, 68, 77, 81, 85, 117, 119, 121, 126, 127, 128, 129, 130
    sanding, 103
Sugar Cookie Cream Sandwiches, 92–93
Super-Rich Chocolate Cupcakes, 52–53

V
Vanilla Cake Pops, 112–113
Vanilla Cake with Mocha Icing, 29
Vanilla Cupcakes, 60–61
Vanilla Filling Cream, 120
Vanilla Glaze, 47, 117

W
Whipped Cream, 33, 119
White Chocolate Cookies, 69
White Confectioners' Icing, 111

Z
Zesty Lemon Stars, 82–83

DEDICATED TO

*Mila and Liam, my lovely grandkids who have been my mos[t]
deligthful and pleasureable gift.*
— Patricia Cartin

To Sally and our Turetsky cousins, who love and know how to enjoy a 'Viennese table'
— Karen Matsu Greenberg

My lovely mother, Yong Kim, who supports me in everything that I do.
— Elizabeth Yuna Kim

Marleen Cosiol, Ofelia Ferencz and Tobel Cosiol, three angels in the kitchen
— Carol Guzowsk[i]